The Complete Boat Angler

THE COMPLETE BOAT ANGLER:
A GUIDE TO SEA FISHING

Bob Gledhill

The Crowood Press

First published in 1988 by
The Crowood Press Ltd
Ramsbury, Marlborough
Wiltshire SN8 2HR

© Bob Gledhill 1988, 1994

Revised edition 1994

British Library Cataloguing in Publication Data

A catalogue record for this book is available from the British Library.
ISBN 1 85223 825 9

Typeset by John Weallans Book Production Services, Warminster, Wiltshire
Printed in Great Britain by The Bath Press

Contents

Introduction

The most profound statement ever made about going afloat was by the Rat in *Wind In The Willows*, when he declares that, 'there is *nothing* half so much worth doing as simply messing about in boats'. Now the Rat was a very wise creature of the riverbank and it is impertinent of me to suggest he was wrong, but there is *something* better than simple messing in boats – fishing in boats.

I've met very few sea anglers who do not like boat fishing. Many find it difficult because of shaky sea legs, but wish earnestly

Boat fishing – so much more fun than just messing about in boats.

that they could do more. Some don't do it because of the expense, but wish that they could afford to. Only a fraction simply do not enjoy the experience.

Boat angling falls neatly into two categories: fishing from charter boats whose skippers take out groups of paying passengers; and fishing from privately owned small boats, when the angler is his own skipper. This book is about both types. It is comprehensive: whatever information a sea angler wants, so long as it concerns boat fishing the answer will be here.

Skippering your own boat offers a double challenge to the sea angler. Not only is there the fish to be outwitted, but you have to learn and practise boat skills since your own safety and the safety of any passengers is in your hands. What a boat of your own offers is the freedom to do exactly what you want, when you want. When and where you put to sea and fish are governed by yourself. If you fancy a few hours on a nice summer evening, or a very early start in darkness to get the best of the tide, you can do it, and be on your way home with the prize while the charter boat is still loading up with passengers.

This flexibility is what appeals to most boat-owners. You almost always have a greater turn of speed, which means that fishing grounds are reached much more quickly. Moving can be accomplished in a matter of minutes and is not the time-consuming job it is with a big charter boat. The lightness of the craft means that you can creep up on fish much more easily and its small size means that you can nip in and out of shallow marks with less worry of going aground.

Charter-boat fishing offers something different. In a charter boat you concentrate solely on the angling matters. You can leave the intricacies of maintenance, launching, navigation and fish-finding to the man who is being paid to perform these things. It is a much cheaper method of boat fishing unless you go out very often. A modest trip on a charter boat may cost £14; a modest boat and engine outfit of your own might cost £2,000 (plus the ongoing costs of maintenance, petrol re-equipping, etc.).

Charter-boat fishing enables you to fish well offshore on grounds that a small private boat could not attempt. You will also get afloat in weather that is too rough for a small private boat. Fish-finding will be done by a professional who is searching the same bit of ocean several days a week and knows (or should do!) where the best chance of fish lies. You have room to move about and there is the chance of shelter from bad weather, and maybe a welcome fresh pot of tea. It is understandable that so many anglers feel the expense and hassle of owning your own boat just do not compare with the luxury of being chauffeur-driven every time you fancy going boat fishing.

It is of course possible to enjoy the best of both worlds – by using your own boat for the bulk of your fishing while taking advantage of charter boats to take on the type of fishing that a small boat could not tackle.

Boat angling is growing healthily. The prime reason is simply that shore fishing does not produce so much fish as it once did. While the erudite among us may offer prose over the deeper meaning and rewards of gentle angling, the bottom line is a tight line. Boat angling can still give blank days, but there are far fewer of them, and quality and quantity are invariably greater from a boat.

Boat angling is not the refuge of failed beach anglers – a jibe often trotted out by the landlocked and based on the fact that the basic skill of shore fishing – casting – is not needed from a boat. Anyway, the chapter on boat-casting will show that casting skills are needed in boat fishing these days.

Angling as a whole is composed of many skills. Boat fishing calls on some and leaves others, as does shore fishing. What more basic skill is there than locating the fish? A shore angler need only trot down to the pier and choose from a few hundred yards. The poor boat angler has hundreds of square miles in which he can get it wrong. Don't ever think that boat fishing is in some way opting out of the hard work of sea angling.

Whichever form of boat fishing you pursue – and I hope by the end of this book to have persuaded you to practise both – remember that safety is of paramount importance. You can fall out of a charter boat just as easily as out of a dinghy. Whether or not to go out, should never be a fifty-fifty matter: if conditions present this dilemma then it is a definite no. Some may go out, have good sport, and return safely – but how much enjoyment did they get from fishing with that nagging fear about the state of the weather?

Boat fishing is all about having fun afloat and using skills that will maximise the enjoyment. That is what this book is all about.

CHARTER BOATS

1 Where, When and with Whom?

In the Introduction I made a gross oversimplification when I said that going on a charter boat takes all the worry out of getting afloat. In truth, it just shifts it to another quarter. You may not have the problem of pushing the boat out and deciding where to drop anchor, but there is still a weighty decision to be made on where, when and with whom. These three questions are the cornerstones upon which all successful trips are built.

These three key points are not listed in order of importance, since all are equally crucial. You need to score on all three if the trip is to be successful. Two out of three is not really good enough. You can get all three questions right and still fail, simply because factors outside your influence foul up: the weather may be wrong, the fish may decide to disappear, or you may make an error yourself in preparation, bait or ability.

Where?

It is a bit bold to say that there is good fishing somewhere in Britain every week of the year, but if you are prepared to travel for your fishing it is not wildly overstating the case.

January is a super cod-fishing time in Lancashire; February and March is the time for record coalfish in the West Country; April and May see the best of the plaice fishing off the south coast; June is a cracking time for tope fishing off Essex; July is the best month for porbeagle shark off mid-Wales; August sees the North Sea fishing really well for cod and ling; September is the best month for haddock in the far north-west of Scotland; October is great for codling off East Anglia; November and December are really good for cod off the

Super fish like this big ling from offshore wrecks are really only reachable by charter boats.

Kent Coast. And many of these areas have a lot to offer in other months of the year. What the list shows is that if you are prepared to travel there is a wealth of good fishing to be enjoyed.

When?

Where so many anglers go wrong is in picking the wrong port for the time of year. I cannot think of anywhere that can honestly boast good boat fishing for twelve months of the year, but the charter skipper may need to take parties out the whole year round to meet his financial commitments. If you limit your boat fishing to a handful of ports and still wish to go every couple of weeks, then you will have to accept that some of your trips will be very lean. The fresh air and rolling floorboards may be reward enough for some anglers but for others it is a frustrating experience.

You must take practical steps to plan your charter fishing trips so that they coincide with when a port expects to produce at least reasonable sport. To do this properly you or someone in your club should keep a log book or diary in which reports of good trips are carefully noted. Fish are quite predictable in their movements and a time of year that produced fish one year will be a sound bet for a repeat performance in a future year. This is not an overnight collection of information but one which is built up over a period. If your charter-boat fishing is done through a club, the log book should be the property of the club and kept by someone with a methodical mind and access to all the angling press.

If a diary is kept then the good trips reported in each week's angling press should be noted down, with the skipper's name, boat and what was caught. If any relevant facts about the catch are reported

these can also be noted for future reference. Reports in the angling press may be a couple of weeks out of date but are near enough to give a good guide.

If a log-book system is used, then each port gets a separate page or two in the book and each time a good trip is made an entry is made under that port's heading with the date and details of the fish caught. I have seen both methods used by boat clubs who specialise in charter trips and the members swear by the value of these systems for picking out the best times of year to go to the various ports.

There is bound to be some information that the press reports will not give you – most notably the type of tide that the catch was taken on. Was it a slow-moving neap or a fast-running spring tide? Only a word with the skipper when a booking inquiry is made will enlighten you about which tides are best. To this reported information you must add what knowledge you yourself acquire through hard-earned experience. If nothing else accrues from a bad trip, you at least know what to avoid a second time.

Making a phone call or two to contact a club in the area you fancy fishing is always worthwhile. You can reach these either through the National Federation of Sea Anglers or a tackle dealer in the area. The tackle dealer is another useful source of pre-booking information. He collects all manner of gossip about how the place is fishing and will be happy to pass on a bit of advice. All I would suggest when ringing a tackle shop for advice is that you do not do it at a peak trading time such as Friday or Saturday afternoons. Better a mid-afternoon during the week, when the tackle shop owner will have more time to chat.

Many magazines such as *Improve Your Sea Fishing* and the weekly papers *Angling Times* and *Angler's Mail* have area correspondents who submit regular reports of what is being caught in their area. Ring up the journal and ask for the phone number of the correspondent in the area or areas where you are thinking of booking a trip. These correspondents are only too happy to suggest the best time of year for charter-boat fishing.

To get a popular boat you will have to make a booking a long way in advance if you want a Sunday trip, which is the peak day of the week for charter-boat fishing. Saturdays will be little better. Midweek bookings can usually be made at a few weeks' notice. If you want a boat of national fame at a period when the fishing is good you may be faced with a wait of two or even more years. This extraordinary waiting period is because clubs often make

repeat bookings for the corresponding date on a long-running arrangement.

It is certainly wise to plan your trips in the autumn of the preceding year, and at the latest as soon as the coming year's tide tables are published. But never be dissuaded from ringing a skipper at short notice – there is always a chance that through some fluke he has got a spare weekend date. An alternative is to take a booking at a thin end of the season to allow you to meet the skipper, gain his confidence and then ask for a date in the prime season.

I can illustrate this demand for the top skippers by looking at where the famous boats advertise: they don't. One famous angling skipper has even an ex-directory

If you have infirm members in your party, enquire about access on to the boat.
A simple ladder like this may be very difficult for some anglers.

phone number to save him the trouble of continually refusing new business – his season is full of repeat bookings every year!

With Whom?

When you have got the when and the where sorted out, the toughest problem of all is with whom. Inevitably, a port will have a wide cross-section of charter operations, from the conscientious professional to the weekend cowboy who is only interested in grabbing your money and conserving fuel.

Unfortunately, the most common source of skipper names, the angling press, makes no distinction between the good, the bad and the ought-to-be-behind-bars. Anglers often feel aggrieved that someone who has sorely wronged them is allowed to continue advertising with impunity. Why doesn't the magazine refuse to accept advertisements from bad skippers? It is not greed on the editor's part, but a dilemma.

If an editor kicks a charter skipper out of his journal he has to justify it and to give a reason may be slanderous. Even more frustrating for an editor is that some skippers are vilified by anglers for no sound reason. A group may have had a bad trip through their own fault, but rather than take the blame themselves they seek to blame the skipper. Often an editor will receive contrary evidence from anglers who say that they think the world of a controversial skipper.

So what is the answer? Use the information sources I have already suggested as a check against the skippers listed in the press. I cannot emphasise enough the importance of this vetting process. It is only the continuing indifference by anglers towards bad service that keeps the rogue skippers in business. What is even more galling about the handful of rogue skippers is that they seldom charge any less than the good ones. Into the bargain they blacken the port as a whole, when the honest and hard-working boatmen deserve nothing but continued support.

2 How to Book

Having selected your port and time of year, and having drawn up a short list of skippers, sit by the phone with a diary and a tide table. The best time to catch a charter skipper is between 7 and 9.30 p.m. Before those times and he may well not be in from sea; after and he will be getting ready to forget all about boats and anglers.

I have a friend who is a well-known charter skipper and he puts a little cross against any new bookings received after 9.30 p.m. The mark signifies his own doubt about the reliability of a booking given late at night, and he is especially diligent about getting the deposit. Even more unsettling for a skipper is when the late-evening booking is made from a pub, with a juke-box, loud voices and clinking glasses in the background. Ideas born round a tap-room table late at night somehow seem a little less appealing the following morning. Ask any skipper. A useful tip for contacting a skipper is to do so in the early evening of a day when the weather is bad, since he will have stayed in port that day.

Party Bookings

Give the skipper what information he needs to form a picture of the potential booker. Tell him your name, whom you represent (club, group of individuals) and where you are from. Tell him how many anglers you intend to bring.

If you have only one date in mind the conversation will not be a long one. Much better to have some choice of dates, so that you can discuss with the skipper which of them he feels will be the most productive. Even better is to have no predetermined dates but just to say to the skipper that your party wishes to go out with him and to ask him which are the best times of year. The skipper will explain what types of fish are around at different times of year and the months in which they are caught.

If you have disabled anglers in your party, enquire if there are facilities for getting a wheelchair to the boat.

Seldom is a charter-boat skipper secretive. Neither will he attempt to tell you an untruth. On the contrary, it is my experience that a good skipper responds well to intelligent questioning since it indicates that he will get a party of good anglers who will get the most from what he offers. A skipper instinctively wants the most competent anglers he can get. The lower the standard of angling of a charter party, the harder work it is for the skipper.

What you will hear from the skipper is a date spread. Take cod and whiting as an example. The skipper may say that the months for these species are from September to February. This means they first start to show and finally disappear in those months. To book a trip specifically for these species at the outside edge of the season is to put yourself at an immediate disadvantage. Far better to give yourself a month inside the dates offered.

It is essential that you discuss the importance of tide with the skipper. You must know how a slow-moving neap or a fast-flowing spring tide affects both the pattern of the fish feeding and the performance of the tackle. If the fishing is slow on slow tides, avoid them. If the tidal flow is fierce on springs and demands very heavy tackle, avoid them – unless the quality of the fishing demands that you suffer strong tide.

A lot of angling hours are wasted by anglers fishing in a tidal flow that is unsuitable for either angling or fish feeding patterns. Allied to this you need to know if the state of the tide you will be fishing is important. This will depend on the start and finish times of the charter. Some skippers will make an early or late start to get the best from the tide; others insist on a nine-to-five routine. If departing from normal sailing times will considerably improve the quality of the fishing, ask the skipper if he is willing, if your party is in agreement.

When you have agreed on a date you must then settle the contractual part of the booking. As the charterer, you need to know what deposit is required and what the final charter fee will be. You should also enquire what happens to the deposit in the event of the skipper cancelling the trip due to bad weather. Most will return it, some may take a while to do so, and others may suggest holding it over to a future trip. The final decision is yours.

Ask how many anglers the skipper likes to take and what is the best number for comfortable fishing. Most boats are licensed for up to twelve anglers but many are better fished with slightly fewer – say ten. It is a question of how much you are prepared to pay for the day's fishing. Will you pay more for more room or are you happy to put up with a bit of tangling in order to keep the cost down? It all depends on your attitude and the size of the boat.

You should also ask if your party will have exclusive use of the boat. Ask the skipper what happens if the trip has to be cut short through bad weather. Some make an adjustment to the price, others expect full settlement. While on the subject of cancelling a trip, you must realise that there is a great difference between the skipper saying a trip is off and the club saying so. If you think the weather is unpleasant but the skipper is prepared to sail, you may well be liable for the full cost of the booking, or at least a substantial part of it.

There will always be the odd rogue skipper who will say a trip is on when it is obviously going to be extremely unpleasant, in the hope that you will call the cancellation and so incur the fee, but operators like this are very thin on the ground. Remember also that if you cancel the trip before the day you will lose your deposit, and if you simply fail to turn up the skipper will have a case of breach of contract against you – and you will be

A boat that is used mainly for commercial fishing and has gear strewn all over the decks can be a hazard for anglers.

liable for all (or most) of the charter fee.

The practice of the skipper keeping part of the catch for himself is seldom seen these days, but it is worth asking about even in a light-hearted manner. If the response to this question is a choice of either the angler keeping the fish or the skipper agreeing to sell the fish on the party's behalf, ask about the terms for this selling service. I have heard several complaints from angling clubs who have allowed skippers to do the selling only to be disappointed later at the money they were given.

Before you give the final consent to this system ask the skipper what is the approximate price the fish will fetch on the market and agree on how much of your

catch is going for sale. If you do not wish to take home a lot of fish you could consider returning alive all those of a size you don't want, even if it is a marketable species such as cod or conger eels.

There is no need to consider any formalised type of contract, since a verbal contract is as binding on both sides as a written one; it is just that a written one is easier to prove.

When you send off the deposit for the booking, include in the letter the details as you agreed them over the telephone and keep a copy of the booking letter. This can be written in a very jolly manner, but it will assist both you and the skipper if what you want from the day is known before you set sail. This level of detail is needed only for

The ultimate charter-boat wheelhouse – colour sounder, paper sounder, radar, Decca navigation and a man who can use it!

a first booking with a skipper, on subsequent trips each will know the other's requirements.

Do not expect a written receipt for a booking or a response to any points you raise in the booking letter that accompanies the deposit. Charter skippers are very busy men, with not a lot of time for correspondence. You may, if you wish, ring up a week or so after posting to see if the letter has been received.

A week or so before the trip you can ring the skipper again to ask what bait and tackle he recommends you to bring. This will have some reflection on the current state of fishing and will allow you to bring all that is needed to get the most from your charter. Again, provided that you keep the conversation brief, a skipper will be happy to give you a few tips on what tackle and bait succeeds.

Individual Bookings

Faced with the fact that charter boats are usually booked by clubs or parties, how does the individual angler who is not a member of a club set about organising a trip for himself? The quick answer is, with difficulty – since the charter-boat business is geared up to complete parties. Imagine the administrative nightmare of a skipper faced with a barrage of the questions and booking conditions I have outlined, not from the trip organiser but from all twelve members of the party!

The individual angler must realise that he

Individual anglers can still make up a charter-boat party, but they may have to
settle for midweek trips.

will have to be far more accommodating to
the plans of the skipper than if he were part
of a party. A lot of skippers are happy to
take individuals out, but usually only on
midweek dates. You may also have to settle
for rather shorter distances than the skipper
might take a complete party, since a good
proportion of individual bookings are from
anglers who have limited knowledge of the
sport and so would not be able to take
advantage of the fishing offered by an
offshore trip.

The solution is to ring up the skipper of
your choice and ask him if he does
individual bookings on any date. If he does
not, then does he know someone in the port
who does?

3 The Trip

For a couple of days before the trip, watch the BBC weather charts. These give wind speed and direction, and, if you have an inkling of meteorology, weather prospects for the day of the trip. On the evening before the trip you must make contact with the skipper for a weather check. He will say 'Yes', 'No', 'Come and we'll see in the morning', or 'It's doubtful; it's up to you'.

The first three responses are self-explanatory. If he leaves it up to you whether or not to go ahead, you must ask what happens to the deposit should you decide to cancel. If that is forfeit, you may wish to risk the weather and go. If he offers to return it then nothing is lost. If he offers to transfer it to a future trip little is lost — he has shown good faith and if you were happy to book with him once presumably you will still wish to sail with him.

Be certain of where the meeting point is. You need to know not only the harbour but also whereabouts in the harbour the boat is lying. Make sure you arrive in good time. If you are late the skipper will still take you out, but don't expect him to add time on at the end of the day because he could get out of bed in the morning and you couldn't.

It does happen occasionally that a skipper is late — perhaps through oversleeping or because of an operational problem. Since you have agreed a fishing period, if the delay has been more than an hour it is reasonable to ask in a polite way at some suitable moment during the day if the party can stay out a bit longer to make up for the late start.

If you are fishing as a club it is usual to organise a draw between yourselves to allocate the position of each angler around the boat. This ensures that favoured positions on the boat are decided by good luck and not barging in. If you have booked as an individual, then first on the boat gets first pick at places.

If the boat is going to be left drifting for the fishing period the skipper should switch sides on each drift, so that each side of the boat gets a drift with their lines flowing away from the boat and one with the lines going under the boat. If the skipper does not do this, just ask — it is no problem for him.

If the fishing is slow ask the skipper if moving would be any advantage. It may be that through seasonal or tidal influence there is nowhere better to move to, in which case a shunt just for the sake of moving is not worth while. Conversely, the skipper may have assumed through your silence that everyone is quite content, so speak up.

During the fishing period, respect the skipper's boat. You have paid for the privilege of a ride and his fish-finding knowledge, but that does not give you the right to abuse his property. Don't cut up bait on the decking — ask for a bait board. Don't leave litter, old bait or fish guts lying about.

Access into the cabin of a boat is very much the decision of the individual skipper. I know one highly successful skipper who refuses any access at all to anglers. He quite gruffly states, with a wave of the arm, that they have chartered the fishing part of the

Ideal charter boats for inshore fishing, with the accent on plenty of room rather than speed.

boat and not the cabin. If the weather is nasty, it is a relief to get some shelter, either in the wheelhouse with the skipper or down below. Do not pack the wheelhouse like sardines and do not touch anything. Similarly, if you are allowed down below decks respect the area and keep it clean.

Toilet facilities on charter boats are nearly always Spartan, which is a polite way of saying awful. Some boats have a compact toilet unit below decks, of varying cleanliness and repair; others just expect you to urinate over the side. If you have women as part of your angling party it is very important you find out what facilities are available.

A well-equipped charter boat should carry a gaff or net for bringing fish aboard, but it does no harm for the anglers to take one or both themselves just in case. Most skippers are only too happy to assist in the gaffing of fish, and many will generally help their anglers with any problems of tangling, unsuitable tackle and advice on techniques. You may get one or more hot drinks from the skipper during the course of the day but this is a gesture only and should not be regarded as part of the agreement. Certainly do not start asking for them uninvited.

Some skippers have firmly held views on the way fish should be treated. Tope and sharks are very poor eating and many skippers demand that any caught are carefully unhooked and returned alive immediately. This may also hold good for other species such as dogfish, or the smaller specimens of any species. Respect and follow the skipper's wishes. If the fish is not normally regarded as good eating then it should be returned – not slung back like a rag doll but released carefully.

It is usual to settle the account on the homeward trip. Whether the anglers feel like giving an extra reward for extra effort is an individual choice. Some skippers politely refuse extra money, others are pleased at the acknowledgement of their effort. The homeward trip is a useful time for the organiser to chat to the skipper about the trip. What went right, or wrong? Did the anglers make any mistakes? Ask him about other aspects of his business: when the fishing is good and not so good. You can learn a lot at this point since the skipper has little other distraction apart from keeping his eye on the road ahead.

When you get into port, if you have got to disembark by means of a cat-ladder then organise your club in a human chain, each passing items of equipment to the next. You will find this much more efficient than everyone attempting to struggle with their own equipment. Someone should act as sweeper and check around the boat, under decking and in the cabin if it has been used, to make sure that no equipment has been left. Most skippers have a large collection of forgotten tackle that is seldom reclaimed.

The last act is to thank the skipper, and wish him goodbye.

When booking a charter boat it is worth asking that your party will get exclusive use of the boat. A minority of skippers sometimes put extra anglers on board.

A BOAT OF YOUR OWN

4 Types of Boat

Logically, the size and power of your boat is determined by your ability to pay. It is natural to buy as good an outfit as you can reasonably afford, on the premiss that the bigger and more powerful it is, the greater enjoyment and flexibility it will deliver.

There is a better way. Before thinking of your pocket, consider first the type of water and the range at which you expect to be fishing, and base your purchase on these criteria. It is wiser and safer to get a craft that will do the job demanded of it rather than one which suits the bank balance. While mobility of a trailed boat is one of its attractions, in practice boat anglers tend to favour just a few pieces of coastline. If you do fish a wide variety of situations, pick a craft to suit the most demanding.

So what do you choose from?

There are two basic hull designs, the displacement and the planing. The displacement hull is what could be called the traditional-style boat with a pronounced keel. The keel is the central spine and it usually stands out from the hull to give increased stability. It is a mini-version of the huge shark-fin keels seen on sailing yachts. These keels inhibit rolling.

The displacement hull sits deep in the water and the pressure of the water it displaces, pushing on the sides of the boat, helps keep it riding smoothly. Because it is subject to so much water pressure, this type of hull sacrifices speed for comfort.

Most displacement hulls will go as fast with 10hp on the stern as with 15hp. Increased power just froths up the sea and pushes the bow deeper into the water.

Because the displacement hull is often open-decked or has just a simple cuddy, and the engine requirements are very modest, it is the cheapest way to get into small-boat fishing. Where speed is not required and the range is not great they are excellent fishing machines.

The planing hull is designed to skip along the surface of the water at speed. An analogy is a flat stone skimming along the surface if you throw it low and fast.

There are two main planing shapes – the deep-V shape and the W-shape cathedral hull. The cathedral is broad in the beam which gives plenty of work space, it rides flat and is very stable. The main drawback of the cathedral hull is that, being flat, it tends to bang up and down while on the move, and bob with a slapping action when at anchor in only moderate seas.

The V-shape planing hull is very fast and rides through waves much more cleanly, though it can roll slightly in a moderate sea. Its narrower beam means that it is proportionately a little less roomy than the cathedral hull.

There is little to choose between the two designs of planing hull, and the thickness of the glass, the level of trim and amount of fishing area as opposed to dead cabin are more important considerations. I speak of the cabin in such unloving tones because on many boats the cabin is much more than an angler would need – boats are designed for a wide market and provision is made for the person who would like to sleep on board his boat from time to time, or build a little galley and fit a table.

A small displacement dinghy like this can be all that is needed for simple inshore fishing.

All an angler needs from a cabin is somewhere to stow some clothing, tackle, boating spares such as rope and anchor, and safety aids such as flares and lifejackets. Shipboard electronics such as radio and navigator are also better out of the way of saltwater spray. The cabin also acts as a buffer for spray and as a weather-break when at anchor. Seldom does an angler want to shut himself away, so even a cabin door is unnecessary. The ideal anglers' cabin is a short one, which leaves maximum room in the boat for the business of fishing. A few boats are made with this shorter style of cabin, and can be seen around marinas and slipways.

The planing hull is by its nature a fast craft and needs at least 25hp to get it moving. Speed is essential for safe fishing far from the shore. The sea can turn nasty at very short notice and, while choppy surf will slow down your safe speed considerably, you have the hooves to get inshore before the weather does worsen.

It is tempting not to quantify a relationship between speed, cruising time and the short-tempered nature of weather, but, as a very broad guide, think of an hour's sailing time back to shore as the *maximum* range in boats of under 18 feet in calm weather, and half that if there is any prospect of deterioration. Make further reductions if your boat is smaller, your handling experience limited or the water subject to special problems.

Think again of the marks you expect to

A short cabin area and plenty of rear fishing space: this boatbuilder has got the right idea for an angling boat.

fish regularly. How far offshore are they? Are there any special problems of turbulence? If you are expecting to fish relatively close inshore, or in estuaries or confined bays, the comfort and cheapness of a simple displacement hull is ideal. Fishing at greater range demands power, and in this case a planing hull is essential.

How big a boat to buy depends not only on its ability to cope with unexpected weather but also on how many anglers you wish to accommodate. Naturally, greater size can also increase safety, but not dramatically so. Certainly size has a much smaller bearing on safety than the number of bodies in the craft. More bodies means greater weight: the boat will sit lower in the water and the engine will be unable to drive the boat as fast. Stability and comfort are also affected.

For open-decked displacement boats use as a guide a maximum of two anglers in boats under 14 feet, three for 15 feet and four for 16 feet. These figures take account of fishing comfort as well as safety.

With planing hulls there is an additional problem in that the forward cabin greatly reduces the rear fishing area. As far as safety goes the figures given for displacement hulls apply, but for fishing comfort you may prefer to restrict the anglers to two in boats under 17 feet.

The most popular and practical construction material for the types of boat I have described is glass fibre, or GRP (glass-reinforced plastic) as it is known in boatbuilding language. Wood, steel and concrete boats do not fall within the size and uses of an ideal small angling boat.

If you buy a new boat you will see

Simple displacement hulls have plenty of fishing room and are ideal for inshore work.

builders offering a variety of prices for the same craft. This reflects the various stages of completion in which you can buy a boat. A boat as a complete DIY kit may be half the price of a finished boat. There are usually stages in between, with proportionally adjusted prices. Kit prices are tempting but do not attempt to do it yourself unless your are – or can get – an experienced hand.

The prices of what at first sight seem similar boats often vary widely. The price is usually a sign of the quality of construction and the thickness of the hull. Some cheap hulls are terrifyingly thin. Grip the side of

the boat and give it a good tug or poke. You will soon see what I mean. Price is also governed by the level of trim, by which I do not mean polished fancywork and gimmickry but the very useful and essential bits that are stuck on the boat after it has come out of the mould.

The most essential extra in any boat is buoyancy. This is usually effected by filling panels or the gap between the two skins of a boat with foam. Air-tank buoyancy is better than nothing but water easily seeps into the spaces and defeats the object. If water seeps into foam panels they too can become waterlogged, but any buoyancy system – even one with shortcomings – is a darn sight better than none. If a boat capsizes you can climb or hang on to it. A side-benefit is that foaming a wall or deck cavity adds a little to the stability of a planing hull. I believe that legislation will be introduced to compel all boatbuilders to build buoyancy into their designs.

If your boat lacks buoyancy, DIY kits are available or your local boatyard may do the job. It is a very sound investment.

Another bit of trim I wouldn't be without is a series of grab rails around the boat, particularly one on top of the cabin. The helmsman can hang on to his wheel, but the crewman needs something equally rigid to keep him on the dry side of the boat while under power.

A common fault of planing hulls designed for powerful engines is that they don't carry enough strength in the transom, where the engine is clamped to the boat. The power of the engine exerts tremendous distortion stress on the hull at this point and a sudden burst of power occasionally rips the back of a boat out. Either you or a boatbuilder can correct this quite easily by glassing in a piece of wood to strengthen the transom.

Buying second-hand is an excellent way of getting into boating. There is not a lot to go wrong with glass-fibre boats that is not plain to see. The criteria for buying second-hand are the same as for buying new, except that you may expect to pay a third less than the new price.

Instead of having a charter boat for every trip, clubs could consider buying their own small boat capable of taking out several members at once.

5 Engines

Choosing outboard engines is a minefield, and an expensive one at that. Engines can cost more than boats to buy, and inevitably run up some hefty maintenance bills.

The question of what horsepower your boat requires is easily answered, since the boatbuilder will give a recommended range. What you will not know is which are the best makes and the range of desirable extras. It is not unreasonable to say that there are no bad makes of outboard motor on the market today. The difference between makes lies in the quality of the materials and the sophistication of the extras.

At the bottom of the range is the small unit, say one of under 5hp. It will be started by a pull-cord and will have an integral fuel tank. The only control is the accelerator — no neutral gear, no reverse, just either going forward or motor switched off. This is sufficient if your range is only a few hundred yards in safe water, but you will long for a neutral gear and reverse for manoeuvring. A neutral gear also allows you to have the engine running before you raise the anchor — a useful safety aid.

Desirable Extras

With engines of more than 10hp you will be thinking about the following design features. Reverse and neutral gear offer the advantages described above. Separate five-gallon fuel tank and feed pipe provide range without the tedium of refilling a small integral tank. Electric starting is not only much more pleasant than thrashing about with a cord, but gives a more even and powerful kick to the engine. Virtually every engine fitted with electric start also has a pull-cord as back-up.

Power trim or electric tilt is a very useful device for manoeuvring in shallow water when coming in or going out. In shallow water the engine must be raised to ride clear of the bottom of the boat so that when the hull grounds the propellor is not damaged. Lifting a large engine is difficult and dangerous as a single-handed operation, and it means that power is lost when sea conditions may make it vital. Power can be maintained if the engine is raised hydraulically far enough to clear the level of the hull. It makes a lot of bubbles, but provides enough power to steer by.

Power for the electric start and power tilt is supplied by an external battery; a normal 12-volt car battery is a common power unit. Many engines are fitted with alternators to keep the battery topped up, so avoiding the need for frequent removal to trickle-charge it at home. Electrics are covered in a little more detail in Chapter 7.

Oil injection is becoming very popular. Nearly all outboard motors are two-stroke in design, which means that they run on a mixture of petrol and oil. The fuel is mixed when the tanks are filled; the recommended quantity of oil is first measured in and then the petrol is added. With oil-injection systems the tanks are filled with neat petrol, and the engine injects the right amount of oil from a reservoir into the petrol before combustion. One of the advantages claimed for the injection system is that it gives an even and accurate mix, whereas manually mixed fuel could have pockets of neat fuel.

Engine Size

The basis of choosing the right size of engine for a boat is the range of power recommended by the boatbuilder. For a 15-foot planing hull it may be as wide as 25–60hp. Why such a huge span, when surely there is a best buy for a boat? The lower figure indicates the minimum horsepower required to make the boat perform properly – in the case of a planing hull to rise up out of the water and skim the surface.

The higher figure means that the power offered by engines larger than 60hp would drive the boat at speeds unsafe for its size and design. Also, some boatbuilders do not want monster engines strapped to their transoms because the sheer weight of a huge engine could break off the back of the boat! This can happen when a large engine is suddenly opened up to full throttle and the surge of power warps the transom and smashes out. I have already mentioned this stress point in the design features of a good hull, but it is worth a second airing.

Finally, a boatbuilder is a salesman and he wants his craft to appeal to as wide a market as possible. Suggesting a huge span of power means, 'You name it, my boat can do it.'

The middle of the recommended range – say, 40–50hp – provides a good baseline against which to judge what going up or down in power rating would offer our 15-foot boat.

An engine of 30hp would be a lot cheaper and would provide power to raise the boat up on the plane. Safe speed is more often dictated by sea conditions than by the number painted on the engine and on moderate journeys the difference between 30hp and 50hp would have little effect on travelling time.

Engines as big as this 55hp are not always advisable on small boats.

The drawback to fitting a smaller than average engine is that in order to attain a good speed you will have to run the engine close to maximum revs. This exacts a heavy toll in terms both of fuel consumption and the life of the engine. It is often the case that a large engine running at half-throttle will use dramatically less fuel than a smaller engine running flat out, and of course there is much less strain on the unit.

The number of occupants who regularly fish from the boat and the weight of the boat are also important factors. If either (or both) is more than average you will need an extra 5 or 10hp for economic running at speed. Two-thirds throttle usually gives a reasonable balance of fuel economy and speed, while at the same time not pushing the engine unduly. Sea conditions more often than horsepower dictate the maximum speed, which, with the size of units I have been discussing, will be in the 20–35 m.p.h. range.

A tachometer fitted to your engine is a good guide to fuel economy and engine stress. It allows you to set the throttle

Having a more powerful engine on a boat means that you can get in quickly
should the weather suddenly worsen.

Having the engine key on a piece of floating
balsa wood or cork is a useful precaution
against accidental loss in the water.

accurately and time sailings, and over a few
seasons it could pay for itself in fuel saving
alone.

Choosing an engine for displacement
hulls is much easier (and less expensive), and
you will find that the range of power
recommended by the boatbuilder is much
narrower, usually 5–15hp.

With so many variable factors it is
difficult to give a hard-and-fast scale of
engine power to boat size, but the following
list provides a guideline. In all matters
regarding engines make great use of the
knowledge of other users. Talk to other
owners of boats of a similar size to the one
you have or propose to buy, and benefit
from their experience of makes, facilities
and sizes.

DISPLACEMENT HULL		PLANING HULL	
Boat size	Eng. size	Boat size	Eng. size
12 feet	5hp	14 feet	35hp
13 feet	7½hp	15 feet	40hp
14 feet	7½hp	16 feet	50hp
15 feet	10hp	17 feet	55hp
16 feet	15hp	18 feet	65hp

Propellors

If you thought a propellor was just three bits of twisty metal, think again. Propellor options are as confusing as the choice of power unit.

The angle at which the prop blades are set governs the amount of bite the propellor will have and is called the pitch of the propellor. In some ways the pitch can be likened to the gears on a car. A shallow setting is easy to drive so will spin very fast but not have much thrust. A propellor with a very pronounced pitch will be like top gear on the car, delivering more speed for lower revs. If you are pushing a lot of weight with an engine at the lower end of the recommended range, a shallower pitch will work more efficiently. Conversely, a big engine on a medium-length boat will allow you to fit a deeper pitch.

If your engine comes fitted with a prop the pitch will be a compromise between the needs of the different sizes and types of craft the engine manufacturer expects his customers to have. In practice, this will be no bad thing, and many sailors use a standard propellor all their sailing career with no problems. It is on the bigger units that the choice of propellor is more critical and you may get a choice of propellor pitches when buying new. The man selling the engine should be able to advise you, but for a more definitive rating write to the engine distributor's headquarters giving the make, size and weight of your boat, and number of likely passengers.

The petrol pipe bulb must be squeezed when starting the engine from cold to pump petrol into the engine.

Second-Hand Engines

Buying second-hand is a tempting way of getting a bigger unit. When 40hp can be in excess of £2,000 by the time all the linkage, electrics and fuel lines have been bought, the idea of slashing that cost is attractive. There are pitfalls in buying anything second-hand, but particularly so with motors. Unless you have known the unit from birth it is impossible to know how it has been driven and, more important, how it has been maintained. Engine repairs can be very expensive and, while new engines are not immune from problems, breakdown is inevitably more likely with an older unit.

Ask yourself why an engine is on the market. Perhaps the owner doesn't use it much. Long periods of idleness are not good for outboards, and if the cleaning and maintenance have not been meticulously done, corrosion and other gremlins could have been given time to set in. Is the owner trading up for a more powerful unit? This suggests that he has been pushing his old unit to its limit more frequently than he ought. Has the engine become unreliable or worn? Is it burning up more fuel than it should? Worse, does the seller sense a major repair job in the near future? Don't expect to be told facts like these!

Notwithstanding the pitfalls, it has to be said that there are some sound bargains to be had in buying second-hand. Rather than buying from a private source, try and get the engine from a recognised outboard dealer, preferably one with his own servicing facilities. In this way you will have some guarantee of condition and a period during which any faults that were with the unit when you bought it can be ironed out.

Another option where big engines and big money are involved is to find an outboard engineer who is prepared to do a condition report for you. It will cost you his labour charge, but could clinch you a bargain or save you from a dog. If a vendor is not prepared to submit his engine for an engineer's report, give him a wide berth away.

The value of a second-hand engine is very difficult to assess. Condition and age play a great part, but little things such as refinements, economy and the reputation of the manufacturer also come into play. The most helpful way of determining the rough price is to consult a second-hand boat-buying price guide. At least two such magazines are published, and both have sections that deal with the prices of popular second-hand motors. A good magazine shop should have at least one on display.

Fuel, Spares, Fitting and Maintenance

Always have on board at least double the amount of fuel you expect to use. All manner of things can occur to make extra fuel necessary and running out at sea gives a feeling of extreme foolishness and probably fear. A graphic example was when a boat came alongside us in a haze that obscured the land, and asked first where the harbour was, and second if we could sell him some fuel, as he had run low trying to find his way home.

Spare parts and simple repair equipment can be vital. The instruction manual that comes with the engine may recommend what spares to carry. They should include two changes of plugs and the means to change them, two propellor shear pins and the means to fit them, a cluster of spanners, screwdrivers and pliers and – the most useful spare part of all – a coil of wire. It can be used for a hundred and one repair jobs and I wouldn't go to sea without one.

When attaching your outboard to the boat follow the instructions of both the boatbuilder and the engine manufacturer. Also, have a look at what other sailors have done, particularly if you see others with identical or similar crafts to your own. A plank of wood spread between the tightening pillars will spread the grip and spare the hull. A safety chain holding the engine to the boat is another good idea. If your mountings wore loose and the engine jumped off the back during a surge of power, it would not be the first.

It is foolish to skip the manufacturer's recommended service schedule. It has been written for good reason and, while some of it may be done by the angler himself, a trip to the marine engineer's has to be considered as a necessary ongoing expense of boating. Not only will things that have gone wrong be corrected, but an engineer should be able to spot potential sources of future trouble. It is perhaps making light of a serious matter, but always remember that the AA don't go to call-outs at sea.

The maintenance of an outboard invariably includes a washing down at the end of each trip to remove saltwater. It also often includes flushing out the cooling system with freshwater to remove any salt deposits. The easy way to do this is to push a large plastic drum underneath the outboard, fill it with freshwater, and then run the engine slowly to expel the saltwater.

Oiling of linkage points and cables is another job to be done after each trip. Keep an eye on the battery terminals to guard against a build-up of deposits and have them well smothered in Vaseline. Marine batteries are dear, but it is worthwhile having a second one charged and stored in the cabin. Rotate the batteries to keep them topped up.

6 The Other Bits

Smaller items which should always be present on your boat range from safety equipment to fishing comforts. The basic safety items you must carry are flares, audio signal, torch, and lifejackets. Three other items that have a strong safety aspect are anchor, oars and compass.

Flares

Flares are not expensive so there is no justifiable reason for not having enough. They are stamped with a 'use by' date and have a life of several years if you buy them fresh. After this date the manufacturer will not guarantee that they will go off, although they usually will; long out of date and they could become unstable and dangerous to use. The recommended minimum number of flares for boats within coastal waters are:

UP TO THREE MILES 2 red hand flares, 2 orange smoke flares
UP TO SEVEN MILES 4 two-star red signals (or two red parachute rockets), 2 red hand flares, 2 orange smoke flares
OVER SEVEN MILES 4 red parachute rockets, 4 red hand flares, two orange smoke flares

Audio Signal

This is a whistle – a simple device, but shrill blasting carries a long way in fog or on a still night. Not only could it assist others to find you, but it may alert someone to your presence as they bear down upon you in another craft.

The whistle is a very basic audio signal; an aerosol fog hooter is much more efficient. Any old parp-parp will give away your presence, but the correct sounding for a vessel under way in fog is a 4 second blast every 2 minutes. If you are stationary the sounding is dot–dash–dot.

Oars or Paddles

For general manoeuvring in shallow water a pair of paddles will suffice, but proper oars offer a greater range of uses. As well as performing the function of paddles, by virtue of being longer they can shunt you about in slightly deeper water, can be used to test the depth, feel for rocks or mud, and – last but not least – are a darn sight more efficient at propelling your boat should your engine give out.

Buy a pair of galvanised rowlocks – either the kind that fit permanently in the side of the boat or the type that can be slotted into holes when they are needed.

Baler

It seems frivolous and overdramatic to advise the carrying of a baler, but they have day-to-day practical uses as well as their more obvious function. A baler is a scoop for picking up water from the deck of the boat and tossing it over the side. Its important use is if you are caught out in foul weather and the sea is coming over you and filling the back of the boat. Slopping out is a cold, wet and frightening business under these conditions but can be vital. The baler can be used for less worrying purposes. If you have launched through a brisk surf some seawater is sure to have come over the boat, and if you don't get rid of it you will be skidding round in the water for the rest of the day. You may wish to swab your decks after a messy fishing session, and a handy scoop will get rid of the dirty water. Similarly, you may want to swill down the gunwhales if they are covered with fish slime and scales and a simple scoop makes the job easy.

The most efficient baler I have used is a cutaway one-gallon plastic tub. These have a handle, are freely available from all manner of sources, are flexible and are light. Even easier is to fit a little electric bilge pump in the well at the stern of the boat, underneath where the engine sits. They are not dear and can empty water while you are on the plane and the water has run down to the stern.

Fire Extinguisher

I pray that you will never need to use a fire extinguisher on your engine, but one could mean the difference between a hefty repair bill and a total write-off. There is a remote risk of fire from electrics, or an accident with cooking stoves, gas fires, barbecues and suchlike, and since a fire extinguisher is so cheap there is really no excuse for not having one somewhere aboard.

Compass

It never ceases to amaze me how many boats go to sea without a compass. Since this book is not a navigation primer I will not go into great detail on how a compass is used, other than to recommend that if you do not know you should buy a book, borrow one from the library, or − better still − find a nearby adult education centre or sailing club that does navigation courses.

The main consideration in installing a compass is that it must be positioned away from ferrous metal, otherwise the reading will be distorted. Since the main mass of iron in a fishing boat is the engine, keep the compass at least six feet away from it. In cabin boats the top of the cabin entrance is the most practical point for mounting a compass. This will allow you to keep one eye on the compass, one eye on the way ahead and your hands on the wheel.

If you think your compass may be affected by nearby metal, test it by running on a course that is known, such as one between two buoys. If the chart says the course heading between buoy A and buoy B is 300 degrees, sail by the compass on that heading and how close you get to buoy B will tell you if your compass is being affected by metal − or, indeed, if it is just plain not working right. Make allowance for any drift caused by wind or tide. Alternatively, ask a fellow boater to steer the same course as yourself, starting 20 yards apart. If you start to converge or lose sight of each other, something is wrong with your compass or its siting.

I was given a tip on compasses by a wily old sea-dog. If ever you are about to lose sight of land, take a quick bearing of the direction home and *write it down with a ballpoint pen on your hand or a bit of paper*. It can come down as thick as a bag but if you have got those magic numbers scribbled down you are going to make it home. Trying to remember them never works.

You will also find it useful to have a hand-held compass for taking sitings of land and fixing navigational course points.

A simple hand-held compass is not dear and is well worth having.

Lifejackets

There are two great snags in wearing a lifejacket or buoyancy aid all the time while afloat. They are bulky and restrict movement, and the angler who wears one is regarded as a curiosity. None of us wishes to be thought of as dotty or soft, so the lifejacket remains stowed away. If the lifejacket or aid is not worn all the time, it should be very much to hand and should be well capable of doing its job. There must always be enough lifejackets aboard for the number of people in the craft.

Buoyancy aids and lifejackets differ both in design and in legal requirements. A lifejacket must be able to position you in the water on your back with your head held clear of the water. The theory is that should you be flung into the water unconscious the lifejacket would put you in a position to breathe. A buoyancy aid does what it says – it keeps you afloat but does not hold you in any particular position in the water. The buoyancy aid is on average a cheaper item but has the disadvantage of being bulky.

The lifejacket is usually deflated. It is inflated either orally through a tubular mouthpiece or by a small gas cylinder operated by a ripcord. The gas type is much the better because of their speed of operation.

There comes a point in the life of every boat angler when the worsening state of the weather makes him uneasy or even worried. The obvious danger of rough seas is not the only one; fog can present just as great a danger because of the risk of collision. This is the point when you sensibly don your lifejacket. But to do so would be a public admission of your fear, and this is a sign of weakness nobody wishes to display. The reverse is true. It takes courage to strap a lifejacket around you when others grit their teeth and say nothing.

I never wear a lifejacket in the course of normal boat fishing, but for most of the time I wear a buoyancy aid – my fishing jacket. A small number of clothing manufacturers who specialise in marine gear offer jackets with a flotation lining in the form of a thin layer of closed-cell foam. Ordinary foam rubber has open cells, which is why a sponge soaks up so much water. In the closed-cell material the tiny bubbles are sealed, and the air trapped in them gives great buoyancy. My jacket is made by Henri-Loyd, but other firms make them too. A look at brochures or a talk to a good mountaineering stockist will enlighten you.

The closed-cell foam material is also used in the manufacture of flotation suits, which are another practical way of ensuring safety as well as keeping you warm and fairly dry. These suits are one-piece garments, a bit like plastic boiler suits, and the foam doubles as an insulation material as well as keeping you afloat. The only snag with these suits is that they are not always waterproof and can cause sweating.

Anchors

Once you reach your fishing mark the anchor will keep you there if it is a good one. There are several designs of anchor and, while they will all work if they are heavy enough and used correctly, different shapes are better on certain types of ground.

The best-known and most popular design is the fisherman's anchor. This is the familiar traditional anchor, which old sea-dogs like to have tattooed on their bodies. One of the two flukes is dragged along the sea bed in an upright position until it digs in and holds. The flukes are held upright by the action of the stock, the crossbar at the top.

The design is well proven, and if it has a disadvantage it is that only one of the two flukes can take a grip, which can make a secure hold in shingle ground slightly harder to achieve. It is still the best type of anchor for gripping in rocky or weedy ground, where the point of the fluke will wiggle its way into a hold.

The more efficient design is based on the plough. The widely used versions of this are the Danforth, the Bruce and the CQR (coastal quick release). The Bruce and the CQR are the most versatile of the trio. This is a very good type of anchor for gripping in mud and soft sand; they provide at least twice the gripping power of a fisherman's anchor.

Shun the folding anchor − it is for little boats in gentle conditions. The grapnel pattern is another one to beware of. It works excellently in rock and weed, but is the devil of a job to dislodge.

Whichever design you choose − and I would say stick with the Bruce, the CQR

and the fisherman's − it must be heavy enough to hold in the worst conditions you will meet. Since all boats are different and the strength of tide can vary around the coast, seek a bit of local advice by wandering among other local boat users or talking to a good chandler. I have said before that people who mess about in boats are a chatty lot.

Vital to an anchor is 4 metres of chain. This is attached to the head of the anchor with an eye-bolt and has another eye-bolt at the other end to which the anchor rope is tied. The function of the chain is to hold down the head of the anchor so that it will grip better. If you tie rope direct to the eye, the rope's inbuilt buoyancy will lift the head of the anchor under strain and tend to pull the anchor out. The chain is not a recommendation, but a must.

The amount of anchor rope to carry depends on the range of depths you expect to fish. Think of the deepest water you are ever likely to fish in, multiply by three and that is the minimum amount of rope to carry. The three-times calculation is a guide

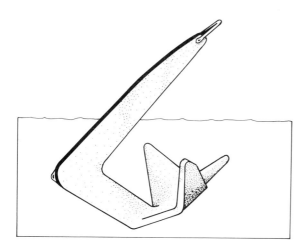

The Bruce design of anchor, very versatile and providing a far better grip than a traditional 'Popeye' anchor.

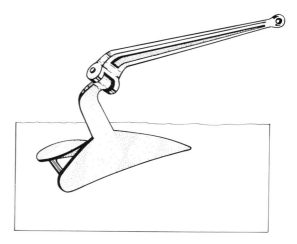

The CQR − coastal quick release − anchor, also a versatile anchor but particularly good on soft ground.

only. If you fish areas of strong tide multiply by four times or even more. Do not let loose rope coil all over the deck. A 7-stone fish box is an ideal rope box, or cut away the top of a large plastic drum.

When you buy a coil of new rope it is kinked from end to end by the coiling process. It must be rolled out and the kinks spun out of it or else it will give no end of trouble in the water by knotting itself up. An easy way of unkinking a rope is to trail it over the back of the boat, but *don't* let it tangle around the propellor.

Bow Rope

The correct name for this is a painter, but bow rope is much more understandable. It is a shortish length of lightish rope attached to the front of the boat and used for holding the boat and pulling it around in shallow water. Launching without one is very difficult. Between 12 and 20 feet is the most suitable length. A spring-fastening shackle fixed on the loose end will be useful occasionally for tying the boat up temporarily to a quayside. This shackle will also come in very useful for helping you haul the anchor safely.

A bow rope is too short and often not strong enough for towing. Forty feet of anchor rope is safer for this.

Admiralty Charts

It is essential to have a chart of the area you are fishing in. Not only will it give you great information on the ground you are over, but it can be a vital aid in finding your way back should visibility dwindle. If you have trouble interpreting the symbols on a chart, buy a copy of the Admiralty guide to charts, called *Symbols and Abbreviations*, booklet No. 5011, which explains every

mark and letter. A tide table is also useful for working out tidal patterns.

A copy of *The Seaway Code* from HMSO costs less than £1 and is packed with useful information on signals, buoys, aids to navigation and understanding weather. I deal in greater detail about understanding Admiralty Charts later on in the book.

Binoculars

Binoculars or a telescope are useful for spotting distant buoys and landmarks. Also for spying on adjacent boats to see what they are catching and how.

Fishing Aids

Get yourself a 7-stone plastic fish box for keeping fish in. Plastic bags are messy and damage fish; to have them lying about on deck is dangerous. Anyway, loose fish end up around petrol tanks and in bilge water.

You may find a rod rest fitted into the gunwhale useful. The neatest method is to cut a deep groove in a piece of flat board and fix it to the gunwhale. Use brass bolts and wing nuts, which are easily removed.

Spare Clothing and Food

A change of clothing is very useful. It need only be old stuff, but every now and then, especially if you get a dousing on the launch, a change can save the day. For the same reason a set of waterproofs can be very welcome. Life is not all damp and chilly on boats, so a pair of pumps and sun cream are also worth packing.

Emergency rations are a wise precaution. They need amount to no more than a well sealed pack of chocolate biscuits and a bottle of pop.

7 Electronic Aids

Echo Sounders

Echo sounders are very useful tools for the dinghy angler. I would put them well behind VHF radio in order of importance, but they are very useful fish-finding and safety aids.

On the safety side, an echo sounder will indicate any sudden shallowing of the ground which might result in a grounding. Also, as you approach shore, it will give you an idea of when to cut the engine and hitch it up. Used in conjunction with an Admiralty Chart, an echo sounder can help you plot a course. This is useful at any time, but can be a lifesaver in poor visibility. If you are heading in what you believe to be the homeward direction, a cross reference between what the chart and your guess says and what the sounder says can be reassuring. An indication of a sudden deepening or shallowing may tell you that

This private boat shows what level of sophistication small boat electronics have reached.

A simple echo sounder like this can still give a lot of useful information.

you are crossing a known gulley or bank, and so confirm your exact position. The appearance of a peculiar rock formation at a certain depth can also provide a clue to where you are.

In fishing, the echo sounder is used to detect the depth, the type of ground, whether fish are present on the bottom or in midwater, the size and concentration of the fish shoals, and even what species are present. How much of this information you receive – and how clearly and accurately – depends on the price you have paid for your set and your own ability to manipulate the dials and interpret the signals.

All echo sounders work on the same principle. A transmitter in the boat sends a ping of noise downwards. When it hits the sea bed it bounces back up and the echo is picked up. The sounder converts the interval between sending and receiving the ping into a measurement of distance which is shown on the screen.

The transmitter is properly called a transducer. It is a small device which is usually fixed rigidly into the hull and connected to the main box of the sounder by an electric cable. The power for echo sounders is usually supplied by a battery – either a dry-cell type fixed into the sounder itself or a 12-volt wet-cell battery of the type used in a car. This second type is the more common, since boats need a 12-volt battery for a VHF radio, any lighting and power start-up on the engine.

The transducer is sensitive enough to tell if the ping has bounced off hard rock and is pin-sharp, or if it has come off a soft bottom that has dulled the ping. This information is displayed on the echo sounder in several ways, depending on the design, and is useful in determining the nature of the sea bed. Jagged rock will show up as a jagged reading on the sounder.

The ping is also reflected by pockets of air. In the ocean pockets of air are found only in the swim bladders of fish. Species such as cod, pollack and mackerel have large swim bladders and give a positive reading on the sounder. Flatfish have virtually no swim bladder and, worse, hug the bottom, so they are undetectable by the type of echo sounder an angler could afford. Fish that are well clear of the bottom are the easiest to detect.

Echo sounders, or fishfinders as they are increasingly called, have come a long way in the last few years. Instead of a fish just showing as a mark on the screen, sets can change the blip into a fish shape. Three-dimensional scanning sets are now available, and, as well as fish, sets can tell you speed and water temperature. Nor are these super-sets horrendously expensive: a set costing £200 has the sophistication of a set that would have been three times the price a few years ago. In general terms, the more you pay the more you get, but there are a few useful guidelines to buying fishfinders. Firstly, beware the glossy brochures which show clouds of huge fish clearly swimming by. The size of fish that is commonly caught by boat anglers is more likely to show as a dot rather than the large arched fish the brochure shows.

The simplest type of sounder is the liquid crystal display (LCD) sounder. This has a small display screen rather like a television. The screen shows the sea bed immediately below and that which it has just passed over. The image on the screen is constantly scrolling along so that as the boat moves over a new bit of ground the new image appears at the far right-hand side of the screen and pushes a bit of old sea bed off the left-hand side. The rate of movement across the screen is adjustable.

The advantage of this style of sounder is

that you get a visual record of what you have seen, and not until a few minutes later will it disappear from the screen. There is no paper to be bought, as with a paper-fed echo sounder. Many of these sounders are capable of zooming in on a particular segment of water and expanding in great detail what is there. They are not terribly expensive. Against them is that you do not get a permanent record unless there is a memory facility, the definition is not always good, and they require greater skill in interpreting the image.

The paper-fed echo sounder has a roll of special paper which is slowly fed past a window. A pen scratches out a pattern on the paper to indicate the depth of water, the type of bottom and where any fish are located. The more expensive sounders can home in on a small segment of water – for instance the bottom four feet of water – and expand the definition.

The fish are not drawn in profile, but appear as scratches on the paper, just off the bottom or higher up in the water according to where they are lying. It is the interpretation of the scratching that is the key to successful echo-sounder operations. The picture is not a clearly defined one. All manner of interference appears on the paper, from such things as secondary echoes, bubbles of air from the boat and dirty water. The sensitivity of the recording has to be finely tuned so that it clears out the unwanted 'clutter' but still leaves a marking of the fish. It is vital to learn the difference between a shoal of whitebait or tiny sprats and the bigger fish the angler is searching for. The best sets cost £500 plus. However, despite their accuracy, their popularity is dwindling in favour of LCD sets.

A final type of echo sounder is the colour sounder. This uses the LCD type of display where the image shuffles across the screen, but everything is in colour, and the colours represent different things. The size of fish,

Using a sounder can pick up the best possible ground for finding the super fish.

the density of the shoal and the nature of the ground are all expressed in colours, and once you know what each colour represents you get a very accurate picture of what is happening below.

This is the type of sounder commercial fishing boats use and the price of the better sets runs into thousands of pounds. While highly desirable, they are not at present within the pocket of an angler. However, as with all electronics, the price of colour sets is tumbling, and while sets are still not available much under £700 they may come cheaper, but interest in them is not very high as yet.

It has to be said that some anglers are disappointed with the results of their echo sounders in that they do not produce the fish hoped for. I can only repeat the advice I gave at the beginning that the results from a sounder are a reflection of the price you paid and your ability to operate it.

VHF Marine Radio

There was a time, and not that long ago, when a ship-to-ship radio on a private small boat was a luxury. It then became a comfort. I now regard it as a necessity.

It is as much as anything a reflection of the care boat anglers now take in respect of

Storm clouds begin to gather while the lifeboat waits for trouble; VHF is your lifeline.

safety at sea. A radio offers several services, but the greatest of all is to call for help in emergencies. There must be a lot of anglers who are still putting to sea who might not be but for the help that their radio brought. Being able to call up the coastguard service twenty-four hours a day and ask for guidance and help is a credit to the way mariners look after each other in times of trouble.

The radio is also other things to the boat angler. You can keep in touch with your pals at sea, listen to who is catching what and where and adjust your own plans accordingly. While the chit-chat sometimes descends to the banal of CB clack it is still nice on a lonely bit of ocean to hear human voices, and if you find it tiresome you can always switch the set to a listening channel and not a working one. Providing that boat anglers in a patch of sea are honest (as much as anglers can be!) the exchange of current

fishing news helps everyone over a period to get the most from their boat fishing.

I must stress again that the real worth of the radio is in personal safety. As well as the lies and leg-pulls from other anglers, you will hear such things as the weather forecast, imminent deterioration, potential hazards, buoy changes, shipping traffic movements in the vicinity, and a host of other public information messages issued mostly by the coastguard but sometimes by other public services.

Regard a radio as an integral part of the basic boat equipment, and not as an add-on accessory to be accommodated at a convenient date. Having made the case for the radio, here is a run-down on what marine VHF is.

The allocation of radio frequencies is an internationally co-ordinated business. There is a narrow band of signals that have been allocated for marine use and the actual frequency numbers run to decimal places behind a whole number. As an example, a marine channel might be 151.456MHz. To tune a radio to this would be difficult, so manufacturers build in the main marine channels as switches and give them a number that has no immediate relation to the MHz rating. This numbering of frequencies is an agreed standard throughout the United Kingdom.

There are about sixty of these agreed channel numbers but only a handful concern the boat angler in his normal activity. These are ship-to-ship and the ship-to-coastguard frequencies. Their call numbers are channels 6, 8, 72 and 77. The numbers in between and above cover such specialist services as inter-port conversations, telegraphic transmissions and private bands allocated to big users such as ferry operators. While most radios on sale are capable of tuning to the whole range of numbered preset channels, these four channels plus channel 16 are the ones that the boat angler needs.

Channel 16 is the frequency that your radio should be tuned to at all times other than when you are talking to another radio on a working channel. The coastguard always monitors 16 and gives out much of its information and warnings on it. Because everyone is tuned to 16, should you want to talk to another boat you announce it on 16 and, when there is a response, indicate which of the four working channels you wish to go to for the conversation.

You should not hold a conversation on 16, and if you try to the coastguard will probably give you a ticking off. Neither should you keep your set permanently tuned to a working channel since you would not be able to hear if anyone was trying to call you, or, worse, you might miss an important safety message. Fortunately, a lot of radios have a system called dual watch. This means that the set keeps one ear on 16 even while operating on a working channel.

You should not use marine VHF for making shore-to-ship transmissions. It might be cosy to have a set in the front lounge and talk to pals at sea, but it is against the rules. The biggest rule of all in using marine radio is to remember that it is a lifesaver and an important business line for professional people, and that while two anglers are discussing last night's television someone could be trying desperately to make an important call.

Even worse than idle chatter is mischief-making. It doesn't happen a lot, fortunately, but there are some people who think it is a great wheeze to transmit pop music over the air waves, effectively shutting down all transmission. Another annoying and illegal misuse is foul language.

All these regulations and more detailed knowledge will be learned by taking the mandatory licence examination. This involves a day-long course of instruction on the operation of a VHF set and culminates in a simple examination. The courses are held all over Britain, in technical colleges or perhaps in a local sailing club. Details of the nearest course to you can be had from the Royal Yachting Association, Victoria Way, Woking, Surrey, (Tel:04862 5022).

There is not a lot of difference between the VHF sets at the lower end of the market, which is what the angling boat owner usually goes for. Since the boat angler needs only to be able to listen to channel 16 and a handful of working channels, there is no need for the sophisticated facilities of very expensive sets. These are aimed at boats working at great distances from other craft, which require more complex services from a radio than enquiring where the nearest cod is.

The important thing to remember when buying and installing a VHF set is to understand how the range of the set is determined. VHF radio waves travel in straight lines. This presents a problem to all but members of the Flat Earth Society. Since the globe is round, after travelling for so far the signal is lost. The higher the aerial of the sender (and of the receiver) the greater the range of radio contact. This is why a lot of commercial fishing boats have the aerial positioned at the top of the mast.

Very high aerials are not practical on small angling boats, and the average aerial height of two metres will give a working range of not more than 10 miles between two angling boats – but a much greater one between a boat and the coastguard, since the coastguard aerial will be very high. This explains why hand-held sets with their little stubby aerials are of limited use in a boat. The power of a set does not affect range so don't think that if you buy a set with a huge wattage it will pick up catch reports off south-east Iceland.

A radio must be correctly installed, but when you buy a set it will have fixing instructions with it. The only final word of advice on radios I can offer is to keep them dry at all times. They are delicate pieces of electronics, containing the obligatory microchips, semiconductors and printed circuits that are so attractive to saltwater. Repairing sets is usually expensive, sometimes impossible.

Electric Power

You will need an electricity supply on all but the simplest of outfits. It will power the lighting, the VHF radio, the echo sounder, the electric start on the engine, the power tilt and any other bits, such as radar, navigator, bilge pump, hooter and windscreen wipers. All these items will run on 12-volt DC wet-cell battery power. This is the system used on motor cars, and many anglers use ordinary car batteries as their power supply very successfully.

You can buy specially marinised batteries – heavy duty, splashproof and spillproof – but they are very expensive. Whether you go for a special or just a reliable standard car battery depends on the power output you need and what you can afford. Obviously, if you get a car battery it must be a good one, not something clawed from a scrapyard. It is a wise move to have two batteries on board, one connected up and one sealed and stored in the cabin. Ensure that the secondary battery is kept fully charged and put it in service regularly.

You will find it useful to have the battery stored in a wooden box with a lid and a couple of carrying handles. This both protects the battery from spray and makes it easier to remove from the boat for charging at home. Saltwater is a wicked enemy of anything electrical. Protect the terminals by lavish application of Vaseline or a thick grease. Bad connections at the battery terminals are the most frequent source of electrical faults. Check such things as crocodile clips if you use them to connect the cables to the battery. They corrode easily and may need regular replacing.

A battery can be charged from the engine if it is fitted with an alternator, as most medium-to-big engines are. Be mindful of too many electrics draining the battery while you lie at anchor. The alternator may do little more than replace the power used in starting the engine, and not even that in the event of a difficult start and a short sailing time. This is another good reason for carrying a spare battery. If you feel that the battery is sluggish, trickle-charge it at home using a normal 12-volt battery charger.

Navigators

To include electronic navigators in a book aimed at anglers fishing in their own small boats would have been fanciful a few years ago. They were things charter boat skippers dreamed of and were so expensive that I doubt if fewer than a handful of private angling boats had them. A navigator is now the thing to be seen with.

The most widely used system in Britain is called Decca. A series of land-based radio transmitters bleep out a simple signal which is received by a boat-mounted Decca receiver by way of an aerial on the cabin roof. The receiver selects two of the signals, identifies the direction of their sources, and displays them as numbers on a little screen. These numbers are like map co-ordinates and by plotting them on a special Decca Admiralty Chart you can fix your position to within a few hundred yards. While Decca remains the biggest seller in navigation, it is slowly being overtaken by global positioning system (GPS), which receives its positional information from satellites and is pin-point accurate without the niggling erratic signal accuracy that plagues Decca sets. The price is still very high, but falling all the time.

Radar

Like navigators, radar sets were outside the price range of the angler until recently. Now the price has tumbled and simple radar scanners are available for £800. While this may still seem a lot of money, a radar can be a lifesaver in poor visibility. It will not only help you to find land, but warn you off oncoming ships. Anglers fishing areas of frequent fog and heavy shipping may well consider the investment a wise one. An electronic navigator will get you home, but it will not warn you of several thousand tons of boat bearing down on you.

Magnetometers

A magnetometer is another luxury item, but it is very useful in finding metal wrecks. The navigator will put you in the approximate area of a wreck, but the magnetometer will sit you right on top of it.

A sensor sends out signals and picks up sound reflected from iron and steel; the control box has a screen which shows how near you are to the source of the iron. Very efficient, but they will cost around £850.

8 Towing and Security

Towing

If you expect to tow your boat on a road trailer your car will have to be fitted with a tow-bar and lighting socket. The law says that a boat in tow must carry a tailboard on the rear with number plate and lighting. These boards are not dear and come complete with enough electric cable and a plug to fit into the lighting socket sited alongside the ball-hook on a tow-bar. The board will have fastening points on it which allow you to tie it to the back of the boat. The boards have a blank space for the number plate and you will have to buy the appropriate sticky numbers from a car accessory shop.

A tow-bar costs around £80 fitted, a lighting board about £20. When you plug in a lighting board it is vital that someone stands at the rear of the boat while the full range of lights are checked – rear lights, brake lights and turning indicators. Traffic police do not take kindly to incorrectly lit boat trailers.

By law you cannot tow at more than 50 m.p.h.; if you were to you would risk an accident – steering and control can be lost at speeds over 60 m.p.h. You must display a '50 m.p.h.' sticker on the rear of the trailer, the boat, or – more conveniently – the lighting board. Most car accessory shops sell these.

The weight of the car must be displayed on the front near side or in an easily-seen position inside. Unless the trailer has brakes, the weight of boat and accessories must not exceed 60 per cent of the car's weight. If the trailer does have brakes the weight of the load can equal the weight of the car.

An outboard motor is regarded as a dangerous projection when being towed along a public highway and must have a suitable protective cover over the propellor. A plastic bucket tied over the propellor may suffice, but the safest answer is to buy a proper padded cover.

Notify your car insurance company that you have fitted a tow-bar and intend towing a boat. Usually this will not result in a higher premium, but of course your car insurance will not cover damage to the boat or trailer while on tow. You do not have to pay any more car excise duty for towing a boat.

Many boat anglers ignore the law when towing boats; a handful are hauled into the magistrates' court for their transgression. If you want to learn more about trailer law and to study what options are available in trailers, contact Indespension, Belmont Road, Bolton, Greater Manchester BL1 7AQ (Tel: 0204 58434) and get one of their trailer manuals. They are packed with advice on trailing as well as a huge list of trailer parts.

Trailers

If you are buying a new boat then almost always the option of a suitable trailer will be offered as part of the package. This is a sensible way of getting the right trailer for your boat since the boatbuilder will be anxious to prevent a wrong trailer damaging his boat or making it hard work for his customer. You may be offered a choice of simple steel construction or galvanised steel. You will never regret having gone for galvanising, which will restrict saltwater corrosion.

On all but very small trailers a winch will be fitted. Make sure that the cable is in good condition and shows no sign of rust. If a steel cable snaps under load it cracks back like a whip and can cause severe injury if it meets the human body. For this reason, many anglers prefer the gentler recoil of nylon rope, which can be just as strong as steel but without the risk of injury.

Whatever wheels you choose to fit to your road trailer, make sure you carry a spare at all times and a suitable jack to lift the boat and trailer should you need to change a wheel. We have all seen hapless boats lying sorrowfully on the hard

shoulder of motorways, abandoned while the owner tries to find someone with a spare wheel or tyre.

Maintenance of trailers is very important. Pack bearings with a waterproof grease such as Duckham's Keenol and use a grease gun to pump grease into the nipples of the wheels until it spurts out. This is vital if you back your trailer into the water to launch the boat since this allows saltwater and sand to penetrate the hubs. It is wise to strip down the hubs occasionally and scrub the bearings and all surfaces in petrol in order to restrict corrosion and seizing up of the bearing.

If you are unsure which size of trailer is right for your boat contact one of the leading trailer manufacturers such as Snipe or Indespension through your local boat dealer. All major trailer builders list suitable sizes for popular boats.

If you are going to drive your boat trailer into the water then you must keep the hubs well greased.

Security

A fishing boat is an expensive item and it makes a lot of sense to take adequate steps to safeguard the investment through insurance and simple security habits. Boats are a popular target for thieves and some of the worst thieves are other anglers.

Your outfit must be insured. Because of the risks involved, the premium is not cheap. The outfit needs insuring while at home, on the road, on the beach and at sea. Check these points on any proposal as some will exclude some situations to allow a more attractive price. Your ordinary insurance broker should be able to steer you a good course through all the options, but there are some firms which specialise in marine insurance and you can trace them through one of the specialist boat magazines. It is essential to shop around as there is a wide gap between the best and the worst.

Go for the best cover and not the cheapest. Boat insurers don't like paying out any more than car insurers do, so some companies make life difficult for clients who claim. As well as the actual boat, make sure that the engine, trailer, and any contents of the boat are also insured. This will include the electronics and any bits of fishing tackle, which are the most popular target for thieves.

Unless your boat is locked away in a garage you should make it a habit to detach any electronic equipment and take it indoors, as well as such removable items as lifejackets, petrol tanks, and anything that could be easily lifted.

9 Weather

Understanding the weather is vital not only to good angling but also to safety. What is bracing for a stroll down the promenade can be terrifying three miles out to sea in a little boat. The look and feel of the wind on land is no more than a guide as to what it is like uninterrupted by buildings and pushing against, or with, the tide.

Get into the habit of watching the weather charts broadcast by BBC Television. They are an excellent guide for the boat angler since they give wind speed and direction over the coming hours, as well as a meteorological picture of pressure systems advancing on Britain. Don't worry if you are unsure what barometric pressure, isobars, occluded fronts and anticyclones mean — it is all explained in lay language as well as in technical. Just listen carefully to what the prediction is.

The angler who has his own boat should, however, make an effort to learn the simple principles of weather forecasting. It is a valuable tool in interpreting not only television charts but what is actually happening while you are at sea. A good bookshop should have such a book, maybe under the section for yachting and sailing.

It is impossible to generalise on what wind speeds make boating unpleasant or dangerous, but you should build up your own memory file of the effect of wind speed and direction on the places where you fish, launch and land.

Another very good source of weather information for anglers is BBC Radio. The waters around the British Isles are divided up into sea areas and given names, and several times a day a forecast for shipping is provided by the Meteorological Office. This is broadcast on 200kHz long wave at 5.55 a.m., 1.55 p.m., 5.50 p.m. and 12.30 a.m. It gives a marine forecast for the coming few hours, possibly a longer-range indication and such information as visibility (fog), rainfall and wind speed and direction.

You can also get a good weather forecast by listening to the prediction for inshore waters, defined as up to 12 miles offshore, broadcast on BBC Radio 3 and 4, usually following the very early morning more general shipping forecast. Consult a radio and television listings magazine for the specific times, as they do occasionally change. Many boat anglers prefer the local area inshore waters forecast provided by the telephone recorded message companies; Marinecall is the best known, but there are others. You can contact 071 975 9000 for more details of this telephone service, but the calls are charged at premium rates.

Local radio often gives an inshore waters forecast, and you will need to contact your local station to find out when — and ask them to start one if they do not. Newspaper weather forecasts are not as up-to-date as radio and television.

Whatever system you adopt for weather information, remember that a forecast is what it says — a prediction, not a guarantee. The weathermen get it wrong by a few hours sometimes or the weather predicted may never happen. Worse, something not predicted may suddenly happen. If in doubt, sit it out. Wait and see if the weather

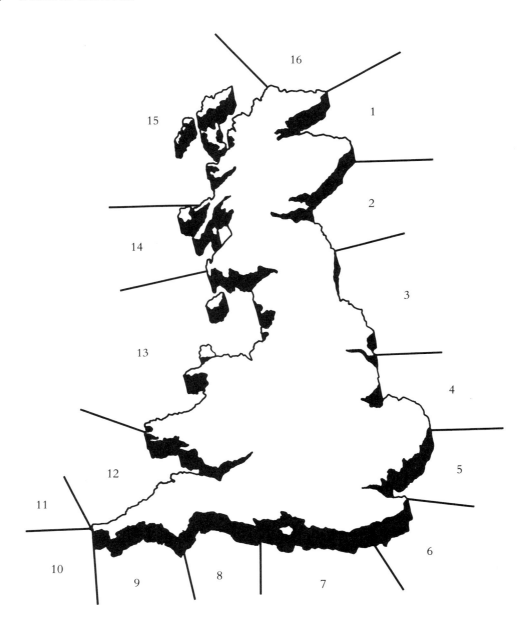

Key:
1 Cromarty, 2 Forth, 3 Tyne, 4 Humber, 5 Thames, 6 Dover, 7 Wight,
8 Portland, 9 Plymouth, 10 Sole, 11 Fastnet, 12 Lundy, 13 Irish Sea, 14 Malin,
15 Hebrides, 16 Fair Isle.

The sea areas used in broadcast shipping forecasts.

moderates. Remember that the sea always appears calmer from the promenade.

Be especially careful of offshore winds. These are winds that blow hard off the land on to the sea. Offshore winds create waves, but since they are travelling away from you you will see only the back of them. You will see little of the white crests and the sea will appear to be calm. Only when you get out will the truth become apparent. The further offshore you go in an offshore wind the worse the weather gets, and the harder it will be to punch your way back to shore.

You must also have an understanding of any local sea conditions or tidal movements which are particularly aggravated by a certain type of weather. If you are at sea and the weather begins to deteriorate, rather than sit it out to see what happens move inshore and watch developments close to shore.

10 Launching, Landing, and Good Driving

Launching and Landing

Launching a boat down a concrete slipway into gentle water presents few problems. The important thing is to know at what stages of the tide the slipway can be used, since many slipways do not extend to the low water mark of a harbour.

Back the boat and trailer down to as near the water's edge as is practical and remove the lighting board and take it off the boat. Unhitch the trailer from the towing ball. The boat can now be filled with any items of equipment that were previously in the car and the safety checks begin. The engine is kicked over very briefly, then stopped. This tests the electrics and the motor but with no circulating water to cool it the motor will be

Joining a club with tractors can remove the problem of launching over soft ground.

Launching from the beach using a car is always risky should the car get stuck.

damaged if you run it for more than a few seconds.

Check that basic safety gear − such as flares, oars and lifejackets − is present. Connect up the radio and turn it on to test. Lift the petrol tanks to check that they are all full. Check that the bung is tightly screwed in. Have the oars or paddles ready for manoeuvring the boat into water deep enough to start the engine. Finally, tilt the engine up to lie clear of the hull so that the propellor will not be damaged.

Unshackle the boat from the trailer and put the securing strap in the car. Let everyone get changed ready for going to sea. Park the car and assemble ready for the launch. Back the trailer to the water, then unhitch the winch-rope shackle from the eye on the nose of the boat and get someone to take hold of the bow rope. The man on the bow rope must realise that when the boat is pushed off the trailer his grip is all that stands between holding the boat steady and allowing it to drift off into embarrassing oblivion.

Common sense and experience will tell you at what depth of water the trailer can be tipped up and the boat pushed off. When it does float off, someone drags the trailer away and parks it in a place above the high water mark where it does not cause an obstruction.

Wade out and climb aboard the boat. In a small dinghy care must be taken not to overbalance the boat; on a cabin boat this is almost impossible. The man on the bow rope is the last in and he brings the rope in with him.

The oars or paddles are then used to guide the boat into suitably deep water. The engine is lowered, the petrol supply turned on, the tank breather hole loosened and the engine kicked into life. The bow rope is now neatly fastened up and the oars stowed away tidily. Run the engine on no more than half speed for a minute or two to warm it up before gradually opening up. Your engine manual may give specific instructions for cold starting, as well as tips on choke operation.

With all electrics switched on you can proceed to the predetermined fishing mark. As a safety procedure, do not let people wander about the deck while under power. A sudden unexpected lurch of the boat can toss someone overboard. There should be a handrail or piece of boat for each passenger to grip securely while the boat is under power.

In a harbour, estuary or piece of calm water, this launching operation is fairly straightforward if an orderly routine is followed. Things are not so easy when you launch from a beach. Few things look so simple yet prove so trying as launching a boat in a lively surf. The boat swings around in the surf, goes side-on to it, and then the waves start flipping over the side. Waders get filled, ropes get tangled as the mariners attempt to push the boat round and the whole business develops into a circus act.

Organisation is imperative. Each member of the crew must know what he is going to do before the launch begins and the whole operation must be carried out with military precision. Launching in gentle water allows for errors – a surf makes no such consideration. It may happen that while the sea says that fishing is quite safe, so lumpy is the water at the edge of the tide that it would be folly to try to launch.

The same procedure is used to launch from the beach as from a slipway, though local variations in the nature of the beach and water must be taken into account, and valuable lessons can be learned by talking to others and watching them execute the operation successfully. The last man in the boat will avoid a wetting if he wears a pair of chest-waders.

The landing procedure is similar to launching. As you come in check the depth on your sounder and when it gets to a few feet reduce speed to a steady pace and use an oar to probe for the depth. When it gets to a couple of feet cut the engine and tilt it upwards to prevent damage and push your way into shallow water with the oars until it is safe to jump out without filling your boots. Take hold of the bow rope and drag the boat in.

Some surf conditions lend themselves to beaching a boat stern first. This means

A pair of chest-waders are useful for the man in the water guiding the boat on to the trailer during the retrieve.

turning the boat around just beyond the breakers and using reverse power to push the boat into the edge. With the pointed bow meeting the oncoming swells and surf, a lot of water which would otherwise slop over the back of the boat will be deflected away. If this method is suitable for a particular beach you launch from then you will see other boat anglers already using it.

Whichever method you use to get your boat back on the beach, someone will have to go for the trailer, while someone keeps the boat afloat. Align the centre of the trailer with the centre of the boat, pull off all the winch rope and shackle it to the boat. The winch is then operated to drag the boat on to the trailer, with someone edging the boat so that it sits squarely on the rollers.

Winching is an awful job, and not the work for those with angina. If there is more than a cupful of water in the bottom of the boat, release it by unscrewing the bilge plug to reduce the weight the winchman and his rope will have to pull. The boat is dragged up to a point where it is safe to connect it to the car, at which point the boat is strapped on its trailer and the lighting board fixed back on, the lights checked and preparation made for home. Check that all electrics are turned off and that the petrol tanks are switched off and the breather holes screwed tight. Leave no loose items to fly out when the boat is being towed at speed.

Safe Driving

To understand the marine version of the Highway Code an essential starting-point is the HMSO booklet called *The Seaway Code*. This is available from most bookshops, some boatyards and coastguard stations. The booklet contains all the basics of driving a boat. You might muddle through a boating career with scant knowledge of such things as safe speed,

buoys, rules of the road and avoiding a collision, but it is much safer and more satisfying to do things correctly.

Safe Speed

It is foolish to think that there is only one speed to travel at – with the throttle wound fully open. This is damaging to your engine and very uneconomic in fuel consumption, and it can be downright dangerous. When there are no problems with the sea, two-thirds throttle is adequate. The last third of throttle will give you very little extra speed. If you have an engine of over 40hp the amount of throttle may have to be reduced even more.

The sea will often dictate the best speed, since if you try to thump through waves your boat will crash down so heavily that all your gear will be strewn about and you risk damage to fittings, particularly electrical ones. If there is a lively sea, shut down to a steady pace, so that you are making good headway but not crashing down. The worse the weather, the slower you should go. To run for home at top speed in worsening seas is courting trouble.

Dangerous Waters

Certain stretches of water will always need special care. Areas of strong tidal flow are examples. You may be crossing a piece of water when you come upon the main flow of a major river, or the exit channel of a bay. Here the water will be turbulent and treacherous. Pass through these areas with a gentle hand on the throttle.

Beware of estuary bars. The bar is an area of shallow ground where the river meets the sea. Because the water is fast and the ground shallow, the sea will throw up surf which can be out of all proportion to the water around it.

Sudden areas of shallow ground

anywhere will cause unsettled water, particularly if they coincide with strong tidal flow. A meeting of currents can create turbulence and something called overfalls, where the water is pushed upwards and swirls in all directions.

Beware of the fierce currents which race round headlands, round small islands and between islands. They can turn a jolly sail into a frightening experience. If you have to navigate a piece of turbulent water, wait until slack water, when the currents will be at their slowest. When spring tides occur, avoid these dangerous areas at all costs, as the increased tidal flow heightens their effect to dangerous proportions.

Overloading

Beware of having more anglers in your boat than is good for either safety or comfort. Inevitably, you do not realise how many angling friends you have until you buy a boat. . .

Determine the most comfortable number of anglers for your boat and never go above it. In practical terms this means that cabin boats up to 15 feet are not suitable for more than two; three can fit in cabin boats up to 17 feet; and an 18-foot boat may manage four.

An open boat of the displacement type has more fishing area and so a 14-foot boat may manage three and a 16-foot boat four. If tidal and sea conditions are different from normal or if you like to fish with two rods these numbers will need adjusting.

Good Manners

Manners are a mixture of courtesy and common sense. Another boat which is fishing should be approached steadily. Watch for where the anchor rope enters the water and remember that your propellor could catch it twenty yards further out, causing problems for both boats. Watch also for where fishing lines enter the water and steer clear of these. If you are drawing up alongside just to have a nosy about what the other boat has caught, you may not be welcome if your engine and boat noise has scared off the fish. Try a radio call if you want to know.

If on your shoreward journey you see another boat out when it is time all boats were thinking of shore, go over and give a friendly wave and wait for the friendly wave back, just to check that the man is not in trouble and without a radio. If anyone waves to you as you pass by, *always* be certain that it is not a distress signal, even if it means going out of your way to make sure.

The ocean is a big place and there is seldom justification in anchoring up within twenty yards or so of someone else, no matter how well he is doing. It is downright bad manners. Remember that after stopping and tossing the anchor out you may drift fifty yards before holding fast. This could mean that you end up much closer to another craft than you intended. Thundering past within twenty yards or so of someone at anchor is equally unforgivable. It scares their fish, creates a huge bow wave and demonstrates what piggish behaviour some boaters have.

11 Navigation

Learning navigation is essential if you skipper your own boat. I will touch on the principles of it in this chapter but to learn it properly you must either attend a special course run by an adult education centre, sailing school or yacht club, or take a postal course. Navigation by mail order may sound odd, but it gives a sound knowledge of the theory of navigating for those who cannot attend a first-hand course. At least buy a good book on the subject; there is a wealth of them to choose from.

The basic essential of navigation is the compass, which was covered in Chapter 6. You really must learn how to use a compass and steer a true course from it. Of the other navigational aids none is more important than the buoy system.

Buoys

A simple system of buoys operates in the United Kingdom. Colours and shapes are used to give a wide range of information.

A navigable channel is the safe passage through inshore water. This can be through an inlet, bay, estuary or harbour entrance. These safe passageways are marked with buoys at frequent intervals, the frequency depending on the trickiness of the course. (Strictly speaking, left and right should be called port and starboard at sea, but for simplicity I will use the landlubber words.)

The left-hand (port) side buoys are always red and may be either big cans or cans with pillars on.

The right-hand (starboard) side of a navigable channel is marked with conical buoys or round tubs with pillars on. They are always green.

You may see variations in the shape of channel buoys, with some of the older-style cage buoys still in use, but the colour schemes are universal.

The passage between the red and green buoys is safe, but you must observe the rule of driving on the right-hand side of a channel. A shipping lane is treated just like a road, with two lines of traffic moving in opposite directions and even an imaginary white line going down the middle.

Another type of buoy you will see is called a cardinal buoy, so named because it marks an important junction in the sea lanes. It is painted black and yellow and will always be of the pillar type and quite large. Cardinal buoys are located at such points as the entrance to a navigable channel, the junction where two channels meet, or an important turning point in a sea lane.

Occasionally you will see red-and-white-striped buoys. These indicate that there is safe water depth on either side; they may also be used as lane separation buoys in a channel. Another colouring is red-and-black bands. This is a danger warning. Such buoys mark a sudden shallowing of the ground, a jagged rock, or a drying wreck.

A plain yellow buoy marks a special area, such as a dumping ground, a sewage outfall or even a recreational area. It means nothing in navigational terms but can be useful in determining your position.

Some wrecks are marked by a green buoy usually bearing the painted word 'wreck'.

Only if the wreck presents a hazard to shipping will it be marked with a buoy, so only a tiny fraction of the wrecks off our coastline are shown in this way.

Admiralty Charts

I touched briefly on these in Chapter 6. Their use in navigation is obvious. You will find them very useful in calculating courses, using a buoy-to-buoy hopping system if practical. Write these courses on a piece of card and keep a copy in the boat as a handy check on the bearings to all your favourite marks. Memory alone is unreliable.

As well as their navigational use, charts provide a mine of information on the nature of the sea bed. The figures dotted all over the chart give the depth in metres at extreme low water. Remember that come high water there will be much more depth than shown on the chart. Correctly interpreted, these numbers give a picture of the undulation of the sea bed and show any sudden banks or depressions, which may hold fish.

The description of the sea bed is done by simple initials. For example, M means mud, S means sand, and R means rock. The explanatory booklet 5011, *Symbols and Abbreviations*, explains these and dozens more abbreviations you will see on a chart. By combining the information about depth and the nature of the bottom with your own angling knowledge of the area you can use the chart to locate likely fishing grounds.

To get the best from the charts you will need an echo sounder to check what the chart says should be beneath you against what actually is. Paper sounders are particularly good at this, since they show clearly not only the depth but the nature of the sea bed. Jagged rock shows up as that, mud has a fuzzy line and the fall-off as you pass over a mid-sea channel or hole is clearly drawn.

Having important navigational courses permanently on display in the boat can be very useful.

The Decca Navigation System

Until the early 1980s the Decca system was reserved for the most dedicated of professional charter skippers, since the equipment could only be hired and this was expensive. Then other firms started to market receivers for sale. After a lengthy court battle, the pirate sets won the day and no action was taken to prevent their owners using the Decca signals without payment. Decca lost a great deal of money on rental fees, as skippers switched from renting from Decca to buying a pirate set outright. The whole system was threatened with bankruptcy before Trinity House stepped in to manage the system.

Signals transmitted on three frequencies by a series of shore-based transmitters are picked up on an on-board receiver, which selects the two strongest, identifies their range and direction, and displays this information as two numbers on a screen. These are co-ordinates, which can be plotted on an ordinary Admiralty Chart overprinted with a lattice-work of numbered lines in red, green and purple to represent the three frequencies.

If, for example, you want to fish a wreck or reef which appears on the chart at the intersection of red line 50 and purple line 100, sail your boat to a position where these two co-ordinates are displayed on your screen. You will now be within a couple of hundred yards of the desired mark. Pinpoint positioning is achieved by sweeping the area with the echo sounder. The transmissions are subject to distortion by weather and are less accurate at night because of interference.

You must carry a notebook with the co-ordinates of all the best fishing marks. This will grow as you learn – by your own endeavours and from chance conversations with others – where the best reefs, wrecks and general fishing grounds are.

The cheapest of the Decca receivers is under £400. For any boat owner who wants to fish particular ground instead of a general area, it is a sound investment. They are also an accurate way of making a passage home in bad visibility, since the first set of co-ordinates you learn are those of the slipway.

12   Anchoring Up

While often taken for granted, this is a serious business. The different types of anchor are discussed in Chapter 6; the three recommended are the Bruce, the CQR and the Fisherman's. You must have at least 12 feet of chain between the anchor and the anchor rope. The rope must be at minimum three times the length of the deepest water you ever intend to fish, four times the length is safer.

You can attach the chain to the anchor at the head, as you would expect to, but this gives rise to a problem if ever the anchor gets seriously stuck. It ends up staying on the bottom, and good anchors are not cheap. A better way of attaching an anchor is by a trip-line device. With the CQR and the Bruce, as well as the hole at the head of the anchor there is usually one near the flukes. Shackle the end of the chain to this point, then bind the chain to the eye-hole at the head of the anchor with a single length of 80lb Courlene.

For all normal anchoring procedures the loop of Courlene will make the anchor behave as if it were shackled at the head. Should the anchor become stuck, then really heavy pressure on the anchor rope immediately above it will snap out the Courlene and the point of pulling will switch to the flukes. This upsets the ploughing action of the anchor and makes it easier to pull clear. Keep a length of spare Courlene in the boat to replace the line should it be broken accidentally or deliberately.

With a fisherman's anchor the principle is the same, but the point of attachment for the chain is the steel eye at the end of the crossbar. The Courlene is used to tie the chain to the centre of the crossbar.

When you reach the mark you wish to anchor up to, cut the engine to tick-over (do not turn it off). When the boat has slowed down, use the steering wheel to position the nose into the tide. You may need a touch of power for this. Lower the anchor over the side, keeping the chain clear of the boat to avoid abrasion. When the rope begins to drop over the side you can let the anchor fall at its own speed. When it hits the bottom, put the boat into reverse gear and very slowly back away from the anchor. If there is a lumpy sea do not use power as you could cause a wave to slop over the stern.

Experience will tell you how much rope will be needed. I quote the rule of three, but with a super-gripping anchor like the CQR or the Bruce you may not need as much. In a strong tidal flow you may need more. The only drawback to paying out a lot is that it is so much more to retrieve. Every 30 seconds or more, hold the rope fast and feel the anchor. You will tell by the feel if the anchor has taken a grip. If it is loose, you can feel it bumping along the bottom, in which case release more line.

When the anchor has definitely held, put the engine in neutral and quickly throw out a few more yards of loose line. Tie a simple overhand loop in the rope at this point, by doubling the rope up in your hands. Then comes a smart move. Have a spring-loaded snap-shackle on the end of your bow rope — the type with a hinged side. Get hold of the bow line, snap the shackle into the loop and

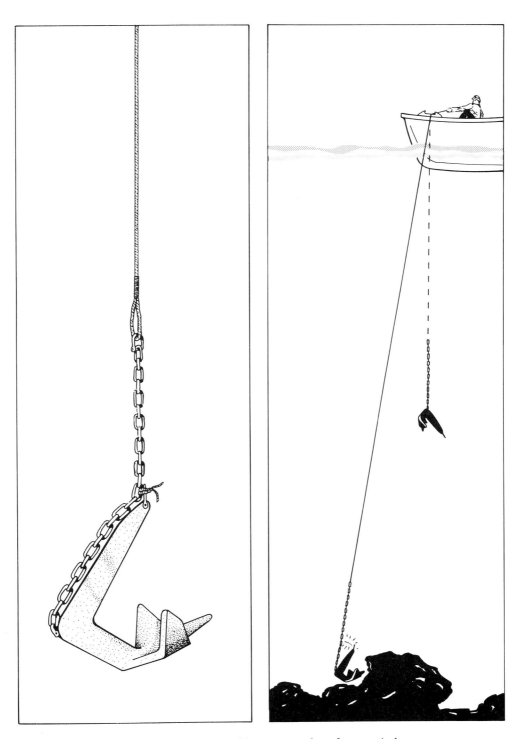

How an anchor trip link is rigged — it could save you a lot of money in lost anchors.

A loop tied into the anchor rope and a hauling line shackled on to it make pulling in the anchor easier.

throw it over the side. Continue to pay out any anchor rope that is needed. Soon the bow rope will go taut on the overhand loop and the nose of the boat will take the full strain of the tide. There is then no force on the anchor rope and it will be limp. Just make it fast around anything convenient.

Why do this? For a boat to ride properly at anchor it must be pinned at the nose; it is dangerous to anchor side on. With a cabin boat a dangerous scramble over the cabin is needed to reach the bow. With the anchor rope shackled to the bow rope, when the time comes to pull the anchor in you need only pull on the anchor rope to take up the strain and pull in the bow rope. Unshackle the bow rope and continue pulling in the

anchor. This is easier to do than to describe.

Anchoring in the way described is all right if you just want to fish a general area, but for pinpoint accuracy you will have to make an allowance for the distance you will drop back between spotting the mark you want and the boat finally coming to anchor.

Any drifting will be obvious because the tackle will start to drag, go slack, or generally misbehave. Just let out more anchor rope till the anchor digs in.

If the anchor gets stuck, and manual pulling does not release it, pay out several yards of line and use the engine to back the boat away from the anchor. Do it gently and the weak link of Courlene should snap out. If this fails, pay out all your anchor line

Attaching the anchor rope to the bow line avoids having to walk along the
edge of the boat to pull in the anchor.

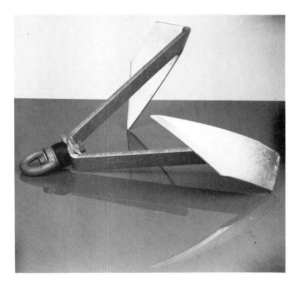

The Sea-Grip anchor, one of a new
generation of 'super' anchors.

and motor uptide of where the anchor is
pinned and attempt to work it out that way.

If you attempt to release a trapped anchor
in this way be very careful of putting the
boat under power in a strong current or a
choppy sea. If the anchor is really dug in
you can quite literally drive the bows of the
boat under the water with a forward push,
or swamp water over the stern with a fierce
reverse. This exercise must be done with
extreme caution; be prepared to cut the
anchor line and abandon the anchor if
consistent pulling fails to dislodge it or if
the sea conditions are worrying.

A final word on anchoring: it is dangerous and often illegal to anchor up in
a main navigation channel. Neither can you
tie up to buoys.

13 Wind and Tide

Wind and tide are short-tempered friends. Sometimes they work well together and at other times they clash to form sudden upsets. The angling skipper needs to be aware of the things that cause the wave crests to rise.

Wind and tide are both forces of movement that can act independently or in concert. Tide run is influenced by the pulling forces of the sun and moon. When these both pull in the same direction the tides run fastest. When the sun and moon are not aligned the flow is weak.

The tidal flow varies greatly around our coasts, both in direction and force. The direction is not that important to the boat angler, but the force is. The tide will run stronger where it is forced to travel over a restricted area such as raised areas of the sea bed like reefs, round a headland, or when it

Standing in a precarious position is definitely only for the calmest of sea conditions.

is squeezed between two islands. Flow is increased where an estuary empties into the sea as the volume of water that has ascended a river, bay or major inlet rushes to get back out. The funnel effect of a narrow inlet also causes extremely strong tidal flows.

The outflow from areas such as these can extend several miles out to sea. In estuaries and bays the tide may well be concentrated in a channel and the flow in these submerged rivers can be fierce. These areas of fast-flowing water need a careful eye; and if the flow is very choppy, navigate them at high or low water, when tidal flow is at its slowest. Remember that the flow is very much greater on big spring tides.

The real danger comes when this water meets wind. If a breeze gets up and blows in the same direction as the tide it will have a flattening effect on the surface of the water and not present great cause for concern. But if the wind begins to blow against the flow of the tide a dangerous situation is created. The two opposing forces collide and the result is sudden and steep waves, which can be very worrying.

If a breeze gets up while you are fishing, think of the effect it is having on the water you will have to navigate to reach home and consider whether any immediate action is needed on your part. You may need to do no more than watch that the breeze gets no stronger, but, while the water you are fishing in is tolerable, that which you have to pass through to get home may force an early retirement.

Remember too that the tide flows in two directions. While a breeze flattens the waves the tide is flowing one way, when the tide begins to run in the opposite direction the same breeze will bring about a sudden wind-against-tide situation. This change can be very abrupt, and the sea can become rough when there has been no material change in the wind speed. You may be wise to head for home while the tide is standing if this situation is to develop later in the day.

Sudden chopping up of the water can occur with no wind when two opposing currents meet. This can happen around headlands or where an outflowing submerged channel meets the main body of sea. This is called a confluence of current and is very disagreeable.

14   In Trouble

We pray that it will never happen, but eventually it does. Hope that any troubles are small and that you have the skill to get out of them. Some troubles are unavoidable; others are your own fault.

Trouble with the boat while at sea should nearly always be avoidable. Structural problems should bring no danger since any faults ought to become apparent gradually. One of the few accidents that can happen occurs when too large an engine has been fitted on too slender a transom, and a sudden opening up of the engine first warps then shatters the rear end of the boat. I have only heard of this happening twice but in each case the boat sank within a minute and the anglers involved had no warning and only just enough time to grab a lifejacket.

Engine Problems

Engine problems are much more frequent, and a jolly life on the ocean wave can turn into a worrying and lonely place when the engine splutters to a halt. That is why regular and proper outboard maintenance is essential. Your emergency repair kit should carry spark plugs. If frequent turns of the engine fail to start up the motor, changing of the plugs is a useful exercise. If the plugs have become oiled up or sooty they will fire only with the greatest of effort and luck. Check the fuel supply. There may be an airlock in the pipe, which can be corrected by squeezing the bulb in the pipe. You may have forgotten to slacken the air breather cap or there may simply be no more petrol left in the tank.

Safety in numbers: engine breakdown and a boat is being towed home. Note the distance between the two boats and that the boat being towed has raised its outboard to reduce drag.

It should be an unbreakable rule that the engine is turned over and left ticking in neutral before the anchor is hauled in. In this way you will discover any engine problems before you start drifting out of control.

If the engine refuses to start use your radio to call up another angling boat in the same area and request assistance. When the second boat comes alongside explain your problem and when you are offered a tow accept it and reward the saviour accordingly. If no other angler is about you must use VHF channel 16 to notify the coastguard service of your problem and ask if there is a small boat in the vicinity which could assist. If there is not, the coastguard will take what action is necessary to ensure the safety of the persons involved. Little regard is taken of the boat itself; it may be left behind or made subject to a salvage order.

A secondary engine is a wise investment. This need only be a small get-you-home unit of as little as 5hp (better something like 10hp) which can be stored in the cabin. A shrewd second-hand buy will fit the purpose, and all you need to do is give the spare motor a spin regularly to make sure it is working. You must also ensure that there is somewhere to clamp it on at the stern. Some boats have a special stainless steel bracket fitted just for this purpose.

If you get into trouble the first and most important action to take is to put down the anchor. This cannot be stressed enough, since if you begin to drift would-be rescuers have got a much greater problem in finding you. It is vital that you do not drift. Better to pay out every foot of anchor rope you have and be certain of staying put.

Fog

If fog suddenly starts swirling in, make immediate plans for home. There is usually some warning of fog, with a gradual fuzziness of the horizon or a brownish-grey tinge to the sea. Take a compass bearing of landing site and write it down before visibility becomes bad. Do not panic and head in at full bore. There is a danger of collision in fog and speed increases the risk of a serious incident. You should carry an aerosol foghorn. Sound it with a 3-second blast every 2 minutes. A spare canister is useful. If you ever use the foghorn, replace the canister with a fresh one as the aerosols do not have a great capacity.

You must listen carefully for engine noise and other horn signals when travelling through fog. To do this properly you must cut the engine to tick-over every few minutes to listen intently. This is especially important if you are travelling along a sea channel. If you have to cross a sea channel, do so at right angles and do it quickly.

Have flares to hand in case you have to attract the attention of an oncoming boat. Never assume that your boat will have been picked up on the radar of a bigger ship. You may be too small to be noticed. Insist that all crew members put on lifejackets.

Fog brings with it chilliness and a chopping up of the sea. Do not panic – the sea will not get dangerously rough before the fog has cleared.

Above all else, do not mistrust the compass in favour of instinct. Journeys seem intolerably longer in fog and there is a temptation to deviate from the bearing. Remember, the compass is unaffected by fog, but a worried angler's judgement is.

Rough Seas

If the sea turns rough you must make for calmer water. Unless it is dangerous to do so, beach the boat. Do not try to beach the boat if there is a treacherous estuary bar to cross with surf breaking over it at low water, or if surf is crunching on to a steep beach at high water. In these circumstances it is more prudent to come in close and ride out the sea at anchor until the danger has eased – when the bar is covered, or the tide recedes from the steepest part of the beach. Sudden pieces of rough sea very close to land are the most dangerous. More boats capsize in the final hundred yards of surf than anywhere else.

If the sea is deteriorating alarmingly you have no choice but to hit land and risk a capsize at the water's edge, since to stay at sea could risk life. These water's-edge upsets are dramatic and usually end up with the loss of equipment or even of the boat, but they seldom result in injury since you can scramble out of the water.

If you are faced with making a forced landing, prepare for the mayhem that will follow. Make sure that everyone has lifejackets tied on, that any loose gear is tied down, and that the bow rope is in somebody's hand. Wait just behind the edge of the breakers and then, just before a wave hits the back of the boat, open up the engine and ride powerfully into the beach with the wave.

Kill the engine as the boat touches and all leap out. Scramble ashore with the bow rope and heave on it. You may be able to use the power of a wave to drag the boat clear; otherwise the undertow may threaten to drag the boat back, in which case the man on the bow rope must let go or risk being dragged into the surf. Just hope your insurance cover is good. . .

If you are caught out offshore and have to go through high waves, use only enough speed to make steady progress. To attempt to travel quickly will result in a severe battering of the boat at best and structural damage at worst, as you clear the crest of a wave, sail through the air and come crashing down into a trough. Thrusting the bow into a solid wall of water also brings a risk of capsize.

Avoid going through waves sideways, which causes rolling and the risk of capsize. Go at waves diagonally and take a longer course if necessary to do so.

Heading through waves is scary and a lot of water crashes over you, but it is nothing like as dangerous as having the waves travelling up your rear. If you have to sail in the same direction as the waves, you will be subject to what is called a following sea. The wave will pick you up and you will appear to stop suddenly on the crest before being pushed headlong down into the trough at great speed. The danger is that while you are in a trough a second wave will come down the wall and flood over your stern. A second problem is loss of steerage. The wave will slew you round alarmingly and severe correction of the steering wheel is needed.

Thankfully, these events are rare, but it is essential that the boat angler has at least a sketchy idea of what – and what not – to do when trouble looms.

15 Afloat After Dark

Whatever difficulties boating and angling can bring in daylight are doubled, maybe trebled, after dark. This is especially true of safety matters. You cannot be seen and you can see precious little yourself. Not only will land be no more than twinkling lights; you cannot see much of sea conditions, and sudden obstacles in the water and other boats will be no more than a few lights.

This is not to say that you should never go night fishing, just that you must be careful and thoughtful. What is more likely than a full-blown all-nighter is that you will have darkness at one end of the fishing day.

If you are fishing in darkness it is imperative that you do so in the company of another boat, and that no boat on its own stays out.

If there is even the remotest chance that you will be sailing in darkness your boat must be fitted with proper lighting in accordance with shipping regulations. These are subject to regular amendment, and a boatyard (where navigation lights can be bought) should know the regulations in force.

At the time of writing, the normal angling boat of between 12 and 21 feet will need a central white light mounted on a post

Night fishing requires a lot more care, but can bring great rewards like this 34lb cod.

or mast and giving an all-round, 360-degree light. On the left-hand (port) side of the boat you must have a red light, and on the right-hand (starboard) side a green light. The intensity, distance apart and angle of all lights must conform to government standards, so get a proper lighting kit, which will have fitting instructions.

If you see the green, white and red lights of an oncoming ship while you are under power in a navigation channel first make sure that you are on the correct side of the channel. Remember that at sea the rule of the road is that you drive on the *right* – the opposite of what you do on land. As long as you are moving forward, stay on the right-hand side of any channel. A check is that the buoy nearest you should be of the same colour as your boat's light facing it.

If a boat begins heading towards you in the dark while you are in a narrow channel attempt to raise the skipper on VHF channel 16. Summon it as follows 'Unnamed vessel proceeding towards — I am vessel —. We shall pass each other red to red. Acknowledge – over.'

You should get an acknowledgement confirming that you are both on the correct course to pass each other in the correct manner. If the boat is a large one then you must steer well away from her course. Do not expect a deviation – a big boat may need the central part of a narrow channel to keep sufficient water underneath her for safe passage. Even if the oncoming boat is a small one there is no reason why you should not swing well wide to the right of it if it is safe to do so.

Always assume that the skipper of an oncoming boat has not seen you and be prepared to take emergency action. Never

anchor up at night near any area shipping is likely to pass through.

You will need a light while you are actually fishing. A suspended paraffin pressure lamp is not that good, since when it catches your eyes it blinds you temporarily. A small gas lantern hung from a cabin door gives a softer and less fierce light. A torch can be used for more delicate work such as tying knots and baiting up.

After you have settled down to fishing, if you have got a VHF radio summon the coastguard on channel 16 and tell him the name of your boat, where you are fishing and how long you expect to be out. If you vary from this programme substantially inform the coastguard. There is a good reason for this. If there is a little movement in the sea, a light suspended from a pole will bob and flash, and someone on shore might assume that someone in trouble is trying to attract attention. If the coastguard is informed he will be able to call you up and check that the light is not a distress beacon.

For similar reasons it is vital that you keep a listening ear on marine band channel 16, the one the coastguard uses. Should anyone be concerned about your late homecoming, or if the coastguard wants to check that a fishing light is not a call for help, he needs to be able to reach you quickly. If you and a pal are discussing last night's television on channel 8 for hours on end the coastguard will have no option but to mount a full-blown rescue.

Do not be tempted to go out further than easy sight of land, should the visibility suddenly deteriorate – and there is more fog at night than in daylight – you don't want to be playing guessing games in zero visibilty.

BOAT–FISHING TACKLE

16 Tackle for Pleasure — and Success

There was a time (some may say it is still with us) when boat-angling tackle owed much to its historic connection with the commercial fishing industry, in which sport and the pleasure of handling the tackle and bringing a fish to the boat have no importance. This meant tackle was very heavy in every respect. Rods were short and stiff and lines stronger than the fish and conditions being tested, and this heavyweight approach extended to sinker weights and hooks. Those who sneer at boat angling as crude are not basing their jibe on pure imagination.

Some things are now changing. Since the early 1980s there has been a movement towards a more enlightened attitude to what is needed in boat-fishing tackle. There has been no overnight revolution, but an evolutionary process in which boat anglers have gradually learnt (by listening, reading and watching others) that to take a gentler approach to tackle brings not only the aesthetic rewards of more pleasure from the hunt but physical success as well – a more refined approach to boat angling brings more fish.

The fishing tackle manufacturers have responded cautiously, concerned lest something hailed as a new dawn turn out to be an expensive whim. It is as though those who make the tackle move as gingerly as some who use it, when they might have been expected to offer the lead.

The new attitude to lighter and more balanced tackle results both in more fun –

hooked fish can flex rods and test clutches – and in more bites, since light tackle invariably leads to greater movement of the terminal rig and a less unnatural feel to the bait when a fish picks it up.

I regularly badger boat anglers to go lighter in both rods and line strength, with varying levels of success. Their reluctance to try is based on the fear that their line will be broken by the power of the fish. The reality is that they get no more fish losses than they did when using stiff rods and heavy line. I cannot recall any angler who has made a switch to sensibly lighter tackle telling me that scaling down was a bad move.

The principal factors governing strength of tackle are tide run and depth (which often go hand in hand), the hostility of the ground on which you are fishing and the size of the fish you reasonably expect to catch. As the tide flows past a fishing line it exerts a pull on it. The line is prevented from being swept away by the weight of the sinker. There is, therefore, a direct relationship between the weight of the sinker, the speed of the tide and the thickness of the line.

Assume that the speed of the tide is a constant 2 m.p.h. Let us also guess that in order to hold the tackle in place on the sea bed 24lb BS line requires 12oz of lead (these figures are purely arbitrary). By reducing the diameter of the line you reduce the tidal drag on it; if you halve the diameter of the line (this may not be half the breaking strain) you will halve the amount of lead

Bob Gledhill with a fine pollack caught on 12lb class tackle, plenty strong enough for this fine sporting species.

needed to hold the tackle in position. At a stroke, you can cut down to 6oz of lead – a transition from something rather dull and unresponsive to a situation where bites are freely felt, fish can duck and dive when hooked and the whole business of angling takes on a brighter feel.

Reducing line diameter and sinker weight is not possible everywhere. If you are drift fishing over very broken ground and continually getting caught up on rock and weed, it makes no sense to use light line that has not the strength to pull free from the obstructions. Wrecks are the ultimate tackle graveyard and I believe it quite reasonable to use line of up to 50lb BS where you are dropping a bait into the heart of the twisted tangle of torn steel and hoping to bully out huge congers.

Lighter line must also be used with caution if you fish in fast-flowing water. You are not battling with the fish alone but with the pull of the tide. Imagine a 15lb thornback on 12lb line in a strong tide run. The fish is incapable of breaking 12lb line by the power of its muscles, but should it turn side-on and pick up the force of the current, or, even worse, get tangled up around the line and act like a mailbag, the line might easily be snapped by the combination of all the forces. This, coupled with a reel clutch set too tight, is a major cause of broken line and lost fish.

I'll press home the argument for lighter line another way. Over clean ground there is virtually no chance of the tackle becoming fastened up on an obstruction. If there are a few rocks about, once the fish has taken hold it is likely that the tackle will be kept clear of the sea bed. The fish is then swimming in open water and can be coaxed gently into the side of the boat for unhooking and releasing, or boxing if you want to eat it.

The desire to get a hooked fish into the boat as soon as possible is self-defeating. One of the most enjoyable parts of angling is the battle between the angler and the fish, so why do so many anglers seek to end this pleasure as quickly as possible?

17 Rods

The tackle trade describes the stiffness and strength of a boat-fishing rod by its class rating. This is a useful system, but flawed. There is an American boat fishing organisation called the International Game Fish Association (IGFA) based in Florida. One of its main functions is to administer a world-wide record list for species it considers to be hard fighters. The organisation recognises that the strength of the line reflects the skill of the angler so they have ten strengths of line for each species. In kilos they are 1, 2, 4, 6, 8, 10, 15, 24, 37 and 60. The close translation into pounds is 2, 4, 8, 12, 16, 20, 30, 50, 80 and 130.

When a manufacturer makes a rod of, say, 20lb class, it is designed so that when 20lb BS line is tested to near its limit the rod will be fully flexed, exercising the maximum buffering effect against the sudden lunges of

A 30lb class rod perfectly flexed under load, but no two 30lb class rods handle alike.

a fighting fish. The problem is that manufacturers do not agree on what is a fully – flexed rod. The degree of response of one maker's 20lb rod seldom matches that of another's. If you were to buy two 20lb class rods from different stables, and particularly from different parts of the world, you could have two rods that seem miles apart.

However, class ratings are the most useful guide we have to the type of action you are buying in a rod. Few anglers have any concern about line class records but by using the rating you can collect a comprehensive set of boat rods capable of dealing with all conditions and giving maximum enjoyment.

Do not believe that the ratings given to rods are rigid. You can switch line ratings occasionally. As an example, imagine fishing for medium-sized cod in deep, fast-flowing water. The size of fish suggests no more than 20lb line, possibly 12lb, and even then there may be quite a hefty sinker weight attached. To use a 12lb class rod, or even a 20lb class, would mean that the pull of the tide would have the slender rod tip buckled over. Bite detection would be difficult, striking a fish almost impossible and the feel of the rod would be dead and most unpleasant.

The tide conditions demand a stiffer tip, so switch to a 30lb class rod but keep your light line. The rod has the resistance to

A good boat rod needs to be as light as possible so you can hold it all the time and not miss bites.

combat the flow of the water, yet retaining the thin line keeps the sinker weight down and the fun up.

The IGFA ratings have no relationship with the boat-casting system so rods for this style of fishing are rated by the weight of sinker they are best suited for casting, and that is dealt with fully in Chapter 25. Spinning rods also have a separate system of identifying their resilience – usually the weight of spinner they cast best.

There are some good rods available today, but still some nasties. Design is a combination of basic soundness of construction combined with individual taste, so my comments on rods are inevitably tinged with my own prejudices, but they are still worth an airing.

For general boat fishing rods of between 7 and 8 feet are the most useful size. Much longer and they can be unwieldy in a boat, much shorter and they are dull in action.

Most rods are in two pieces. Traditionally, the join was at the reel seat, with a heavy brass fitting that is now completely outdated. There was a fear that the spigot type of join would not be strong enough for boat fishing (the commercial tackle hang-up again), yet when spigots withstand the rigours of 200-yard beachcasting who can say that they are not up to knocking out a few codling? The reel seat on today's better boat rods is made from lighter materials such as tough nylon or even carbon fibre, with the amount of metal used kept to a minimum.

How many rods you need for your boat fishing depends on the level at which you wish to pursue the sport and the variety of the types of boat fishing you do. If you have only one boat rod and want it to cover most eventualities, then get a 30lb class rod. This will be too heavy for much of your fishing, but what holds a lot holds a little.

A second rod should be a 20lb class rod, and with this pair you can enjoyably tackle most of the fishing on offer in the British Isles. Additional rods are used for specialist techniques, but are still very desirable. The rods described below are not given in any order of priority since that depends on what fishing you do, but I cannot see many anglers wanting anything outside the list.

12lb Class Rod

This rod will offer great fun with medium-sized fish in water that is not snag-ridden or subject to a deep, fast-flowing tide. It will handle most flatfish and roundfish that don't go too far above 10lb in weight.

6lb Class Rod

You will have great difficulty in buying a rod actually flagged for this class of line, so look instead for a freshwater rod with a test curve rating of about 1lb. You can use this rod for float fishing, casting light lures such as rubber eels, freelining bait, or bottom fishing for fish such as plaice, flounders, whiting and codling where there is not a great deal of depth or flow to the water.

50lb Class Rod

If you intend wreck fishing for fish such as conger and ling lying deep in the heart of a rusty hulk, you will need the brute force of this rod to bully them out. Those who wish to drift wrecks with multiple lure rigs will also need a rod and line of this strength to withstand the opposing diving force of two or even three double-figure fish.

The one function it is not needed for is that which it is most commonly associated with – shark fishing. For blue shark and medium-sized porbeagles, 30lb class tackle is sufficient, since when hooked these fish swim freely in the upper level of the sea where there are no snags to cause problems. First-timers in shark fishing may feel

A 6lb class rod and light spinning reel: great fun with medium-sized plaice like this one from the estuary at Salcombe.

happier with 50lb class tackle, but once a couple of fish have been beaten the urge to drop to 30lb class will rise.

Wire-Line Rod

This is an underrated style of fishing and one that is wrongly consigned to the middle reaches of the English Channel. A basic wire rod is a 30lb class blank with the vital addition of a tip roller ring and the desirable addition of side-ring rollers.

Wire line will slice through normal rod rings like a cheese-cutter. Even rings which profess to have coatings fit for moon rockets will become grooved in a remarkably short time – as little as one fishing session. When nylon line passes over these little grooves they will shred it.

The best rollers are made by the British firm Hopkins & Holloway and marketed under the Seymo badge. The American-made Aftco rollers are also first-class. I would not fit any other but these two types on a wire rod of mine.

Boat-Casting Rods

It is remarkable how much mistrust still attaches to this system of boat fishing. It gained its popularity in the waters off the Thames estuary, and for many it should remain there. That is a mistaken view. The method has application all over Britain, as I shall explain in Chapter 25.

The most suitable length for a boat-casting rod is 9½ feet. More than that, and the rod becomes cumbersome to cast, particularly on a small boat; any shorter, and there is insufficient power to cast the tackle far enough. The standard of boat-casting rods is very variable – this is a very British way of fishing, so rods produced on the other side of the world begin with a disadvantage. I particularly like Daiwa uptide rods as complete products, but the two British manufacturers, Conoflex and Zipplex, have excellent blanks should you want to build an uptide rod yourself.

Since casting is one of the prime purposes of a boat-casting rod its rating is by ounces of lead. If you do a lot of boat-casting you will need two rods, one rated 4–6oz and the other 6–8oz. If you want to restrict yourself to one, get the 4–6oz.

A rare sight – a huge wreck left dry by the receding tide shows why such heavy tackle is needed for wrecking.

You can quite successfully modify a little-used beach-casting rod, provided that its action is fast-taper and suitable for long-distance casting. Without the length to assist in distance casting, the action of the blank must be spot on. If you do modify a beach rod, cut the surplus length from the butt and reposition the reel fitting.

Spinning Rod

You can use your 6lb class rod to double as a spinner or you may prefer a purpose-built rod. Most lures used in the sea weigh between ½ – 1½oz, so go for a rod that is advertised as casting around 1oz. Rods designed for pike or salmon spinning will also have the right type of action.

Pirk-Fishing Rod

If you do a lot of heavy pirk fishing, with lures of 1lb or more fished in deep water over wrecks, a rod specially designed for the rigorous work is very useful. Since you will not be able to buy one of these rods ready made, or even described as suitable for this purpose, I will describe my own. It is the 8-foot tip section of a North Western Blanks Ltd backcasting blank, designed for casting 8oz of lead by the backcasting style, which demands a very stiff rod. It has very little give in it so when a 1lb pirk is being worked in over 30 fathoms of water the tip does not collapse and bend excessively. With such a stiff rod a 2-foot lift of the rod tip is translated into a similar lift at the lure.

Rays are a favourite target for the boat-casting technique.

If you intend doing a lot of pirk fishing a special rod is needed for this very tough form of boat fishing.

The reel fitting is positioned much nearer the butt than with a normal rod. The weight of a reel, which by the nature of this style of fishing will be quite heavy, counterbalances the pull on the tip from the lure and makes the working of such a heavy lure easier.

This rod has no pretensions to finesse but is unbeatable at deep-water pirking with heavy lures. Since it is one-piece there is no chance of the rod collapsing at the spigot no matter what the stress; there is none.

If you wish to make up a rod of your own, blanks such as Conoflex, North Western and Zipplex offer excellent models, and the tackle dealer who sells you the blank should be able to fit you up with suitable fittings.

18   Reels

I invited the reader to make his selection from the list of rods according to the type of fishing he does; the reel list is also comprehensive – make your selection to match the rods and style of fishing you intend to do.

Three types of reel are available – the multiplier, the fixed-spool and the centrepin. The centrepin is not much used in sport fishing, though a few boat anglers still like the 1:1 ratio of a big wooden Scarborough-type reel for hauling up strings of fish taken on very heavy line and jigs. The fixed-spool has even less place in boat fishing since the manner and speed of its retrieval makes it very difficult to use in a boat for anything other than the purpose for which it was designed: spinning.

Multiplier reels do not have class ratings as rods do, but they do fall into three broad groups: heavyweight, middleweight and flyweight.

At the heavy end, if you are going wreck fishing with a 50lb class rod and line to match then you will need a reel whose internal organs will not be torn apart by the stress such heavy tackle can impose. Some reel makers in the tough end of the reel market conform to a useful size-rating system.

The system used by the American firm Penn set the benchmark for those which followed. The rating is indicated by a number followed by an oblique stroke followed by a zero. Curiously, it is the same system as used for hooks, yet a 6/0 hook has no relationship to a 6/0 reel. Daiwa's numbering system is a thinly-veiled version of the Penn system. Shakespeare's system takes much more thought to work out, but both of these major reel manufacturers use the last three digits of the reel number to indicate a progressive rise in size and capacity. The Mitchell 624 is approximately equivalent to a 3/0 reel, but this cannot be deduced from its number.

Heavyweight Reels

Reels from 3/0 to 6/0 (and other makers' equivalent sizes) constitute the heavy end of the range; they have the power and strength to cope with lines of between 30 and 50lb. A 6/0 reel is the absolute maximum for British fishing requirements, and many will find a reel as heavy as this most unpleasant to use. I would suggest that a 4/0 reel is the heaviest reel you need.

Since reels of this class are used for bullying fish rather than gentle persuasion, a basic low-geared version is preferable to a high-speed retrieve. High speed invariably entails greater stress on the gears in a situation where stress is already in plentiful supply.

Middleweight Reels

The middleweight section of the multiplier market is swamped with choice. These reels are designed for use with 20 and 30lb class rods, and since these rods make up probably 75 per cent of the market it is inevitable that there should be such choice.

The /0 system still applies for those reels

Making huge hauls of fish like this calls for reels capable of withstanding a lot of punishment.

which use it – ranging from 1/0 to the crossover size of 3/0 – but major reel firms such as Abu, Mitchell and Shimano don't adhere to it and a huge range of Penn multipliers in this category carry names or numbers which give no obvious guide to where in the frame they fit. You can use line capacity as a guide, but I shall cheat a bit and pick two of the most popular boat reels in Britain, familiar to nearly all, and offer them as a visual guide to what constitutes the middle ground in reel size.

I offer the Abu 7000 series as the lower end and the Abu 9000 series as the upper end. I am not particularly elevating these two reels to any superior position over their rivals (though they are among the best), but side by side these two reels give a clear picture of what I mean by middleweight reels suitable for 20 and 30lb rods.

Magnetic braking systems are widely available these days, not only on small casting reels but on larger middleweight reels. They are useful, but the magnetic brake system offers no advantage over conventional brake-block or spool-tension systems for boat fishing.

Flyweight Reels

Rods in the lightweight range – between 20lb and 6lb – require multipliers at the smallest end of the market. This is the type more usually associated with beachcasting, typified by the Abu 6000 range. The market is dominated by Abu, but Daiwa have their Millionaire reels and a couple of the other major reel manufacturers produce reels in this size range. It is possible to buy reels a size smaller than the Abu 6000 if you like the idea of a very small reel.

The thing to look for is the quality of construction and the steps taken during manufacture to guard against saltwater corrosion. Reels are made with a global market in view, and a lot of the small multipliers are not aimed at saltwater anglers but freshwater anglers, for whom corrosion is not a major worry. Abu take special precautions with some of their reels by proofing the finish against rapid corrosion.

For spinning you can use a finely tuned small multiplier but it is so much simpler to use a fixed-spool reel. There is a huge range to choose from at prices which start unbelievably low. Which to choose depends on your budget and the level of sophistication you want, but really first-class spinning reels are available for under £30.

Since you will seldom be casting lures of more than 1oz, and the rod is light in construction, go for a middle-size reel, certainly not one of the bigger sizes which will have a capacity and weight far in excess of your requirements.

Spools

If you want to do wire-line fishing with a rod of 30lb class rating a reel with a metal spool is essential, the narrower the better and without a level wind mechanism. The best reel of all is the Penn Mariner 349. This is a robust version of the Mariner 49M and worth the extra money. This reel apart, most reels around the 3/0 size will do.

Spare spools do not usually concern boat anglers, but they do offer a useful way of saving on the cost of buying several reels as well as providing the flexibility of several line thicknesses and strengths. The only disadvantage is that so few reels of boat-fishing size have the facility of quick spool

change. On all heavyweight and a good proportion of middleweight multipliers changing a spool involves removing six or more screws, which is no problem at home but the devil of a job on the deck of a pitching boat without losing one. All the small-size multipliers feature an easy take-apart facility. There is little point in carrying a spare spool purely for convenience of replacing line when a substantial amount is lost. It is safer and quicker to carry a bulk spool of spare line and wind it on the multiplier.

Maintenance

Whatever reel you have, remember what a hostile environment the sea is. Manufacturers take varying measures to protect your reel from salt corrosion, but none will keep it out entirely.

The main enemy of a reel is not the spray that bounces over the side of the boat or trickles on to the reel from the line being wound in, but the tardiness of anglers who when they return home leave that salt on the reel to dry and set to work. Cleaning reels is a bind, particularly at the end of the day, but the consequences of not doing so are certainly a shorter reel life and possibly a sudden failure at a crucial moment. Even if you are disinclined to clean reels at the end of a long day, do it the next day. Rinse the reel off under warm water and then put it somewhere to dry. Wipe the metalwork down with a rag containing a trace of light oil. Periodically, strip the reel apart to reveal the spool, clean the parts you normally don't see and oil the inside of the spool. An old toothbrush is a very useful aid to cleaning awkward corners.

If a fault develops you can return the reel to the importing firm through the tackle shop which sold it to you. The servicing of reels is not a cheap business if you do it through the manufacturer, and you may be able to get a first-class job done through your local tackle dealer. If you wish to do a repair yourself spare parts can be had through your tackle dealer or direct from the importer, though this will not be cheaper than ordering through your tackle

shop. Penn and Abu do not do their own servicing or spare parts supply. For Abu the agency to contact is Tightlines Service, 55 Croft Street, Lincoln, (Tel: 0522 23834). For Penn it is Penn Servicing, 33 Farleigh Road, Abbey Estate, Pershore, Worcester-shire, (Tel: 0386 552949).

19 Hook, Line and Sinker

You will need a tackle box, which need not be large but should contain a little of everything you are likely to need in the course of your day's fishing. Remember that for a boat angler the variety of fish and fishing styles is likely to be far greater than for the beach angler, so be prepared.

As well as the water that may fall from the sky, an inordinate amount can reach your tackle from the foaming main, so your box needs to be sturdy and as waterproof as possible. While the sea may not bounce over while a boat is at anchor or on a slow drift, once it gets under power and punches into the surf waves can crash over the side, sending tackle boxes flying.

My number one container is a fibreglass box with a weather-sealed lip and non-corrosive snap fasteners. All-plastic boxes are another corrosion beater, although they can be a bit flimsy. A box of a substantial size enables you to avoid spreading your tackle about on the deck, which can be dangerous as well as untidy.

Make sure that your box's carrying strap is good and strong. I once watched an angler sling his box over his shoulder and climb up the cat-ladder from the boat to the quayside. He almost reached the top and the strap snapped. The box hit the side of the boat with a crash (which made the skipper none too pleased), smashed in half and spewed the contents in the boat and in the water. By the law that governs these things, what fell into the boat was cheap odds and sods; all his reels and more expensive items disappeared in the harbour, where they are to this day.

Inside your main box keep as much of your tackle as possible in waterproof boxes of their own, particularly items such as hooks and swivels, which are so prone to rusting. There are so many plastic tubs around that are free or nearly so that nobody should have any trouble in getting some.

Where space is at a premium on a small boat it is best to keep all the tackle neatly stored in one box.

This micro-photograph of hook points shows the difference between a hook sharpened on a stone before use and one straight from the packet.

Clubs will find it useful to have their own set of scales on board so that fish can be weighed and returned alive if not wanted.

Hooks

There is no need to carry a small tackle shop's supply of hooks but you do need to carry a range of sizes and patterns. The make and style of hook has some importance, but if you want to solve all your hook requirements in one go just buy a box of 50 Mustad 79515 hooks in sizes from 2 to 6/0 for everything but tope and conger, for which you want 8/0 O'Shaughnessy hooks.

If you want to be a little more selective, I highly recommend the Cox and Rawle Uptide hooks, which are suitable for all light-to-medium forms of boat fishing. If

you want a very sharp, slightly finer-wired hook, then the Kamasan Aberdeen range is excellent. If you want a strong but thinner-wired hook than the 8/0 O'Shaughnessy, the Partridge Flashpoint range is excellent.

If I seem a bit dismissive about the brand and pattern of fish hook it is a complacency brought on by the fact that the overall standard of manufacture is very good. Firms like Mustad, Partridge, Kamasan, VMC and Au Lion d'Or don't make bad hooks. Since these firms sell 99 per cent of all hooks sold in Britain, even if not always under their own label, my confidence is not misplaced. Whatever brand you choose, you are likely to need the following.

For small flatties, mackerel, garfish, and any little fish you may want to catch size 2 hooks will serve.

For whiting, dogs, larger plaice and little codling you will want 1/0 hooks, and a few 2/0 and 3/0 Aberdeen patterns are useful for nicking sandeels lightly.

For rays, medium cod, spurdog, smooth hound and fish of this size hooks from 3/0 to 5/0 are ideal. For bigger fish or bigger baits, 5/0 and 6/0 hooks are needed. While 8/0 is a benchmark for tope and conger, you may drop to 6/0 for small eels, or go up to 10/0 for large whole fish baits intended for tope or shark.

Sinkers

You don't need a lot of sinkers but a selection of weights is needed. Have a few little 1oz bombs, and a few 2oz, 4oz, 6oz and 8oz sinkers. Local conditions may dictate the use of heavier weights, in which case step up in 4oz divisions, casting your own sinkers from nothing up to 2lb according to the amount of lead you pour in.

There is an easy way of doing this. By trial and error, make bell weights of 12oz, 1lb, 1¼lb and 1½lb. When the sinkers are cold, drop each into the mould and score the inside of the mould heavily around it to mark the level of molten lead required. This simplifies the job of casting more weights of the desired sizes. (Some moulds come with these graduations already marked.) Finally, weight selection is much easier if each sinker is marked with its weight with a fine brush in full of gloss paint. (Try DCA Moulds of Cardiff for torpedo-shaped sinkers of up to 1½lb.)

I am an unashamed fan of the watch-weight pattern, the one that looks like a Polo mint. I cast my own from moulds from 2oz to 8oz, and find them a very versatile design. They grip slightly, do not tumble along the sea bed like a bomb shape and do not spin in the water during the retrieve.

An excellent shape for deep water where a heavier weight is needed is the DCA 10oz Supazoom. This mould is available in one size only but with its streamlined shape the sinker descends through the water much quicker than the bell-shape pattern.

For boat-casting you will need a selection of the wired sinkers described in Chapter

25. For very light fishing and spinning, some drilled bullet weights, barrel weights and spiral sinkers are needed. A tub of assorted split shot is needed for float fishing. The use of lead by sea plays no part in the swan-death controversy, but you will find it extremely difficult to get supplies of lead shot – which is a pity, because the substitute shot is extremely expensive.

Line

Much nonsense is talked about nylon line. Preferred breaking strains for rods of different classes are given in Chapter 17 but these are not rigid. A 50lb class rod will perform well with line from 35 to 50lb; a 30lb rod will work pleasantly with line from 23 to 30lb (try 28lb BS as a starter), and 15 or 18lb breaking strain line is about right for a 20lb class rod.

The brand doesn't really matter. There are few bad lines – only bad knots and bad practices on the part of the anglers who use them. Nevertheless, do not test such a bold statement by buying the cheapest and least known line you can find to prove me wrong. If you stick with the familiar brands you will not go far wrong.

Replace the lines regularly, at least twice a year if you fish regularly, and never use knotted line. Strip the last few yards of line off frequently and bin it, since it is this final section that takes the strain. If every you feel a nick, see a furry surface or glazed look on the line throw it away immediately. It has become damaged and could snap at a load much less than you expect.

If a line snaps it is more likely to be the result of neglect than a manufacturing fault – unless, of course you have failed to set the slipping clutch on your reel correctly. The easy way to get this right is to tighten the drag and yank violently at the line, trying to break it. If you do snap it, turn the clutch back at least one turn, better two turns. Do this clutch test regularly to avoid the day when a fish breaks your line not because of its power but because of your lack of diligence.

There is no real use for braided Dacron lines any more. Their advantage is their lack of stretch, which is very useful in deep-water fishing when the spongy nature of nylon makes bite-detection and striking more difficult. The overriding flaw with Dacron is that it is thicker than other lines and requires more lead to hold bottom. If it tangles it is the devil's own job to unravel.

Swivels

A modest selection of plain and link swivels is needed for general trace making. Berkley are the best and, while they are dear compared with competitors, losses are slight in boat fishing so there is no need to compromise. A box of 2/0 split rings and a selection of drilled beads are also useful.

Oddments

A sharp knife is needed for gutting fish, cutting bait and any other odd uses. A pair of nail clippers is handy for trimming knots and cutting line.

If you are in your own boat, a large landing net is almost always a less risky way of boating a fish than gaffing. On a charter boat the skipper will take care of the final landing of the fish, usually with a gaff. If you want to return the fish alive ask the skipper not to gaff them. You can either risk lifting the fish into the boat or carry a large landing net with you. Few boats have a landing net on board. A pair of thick industrial gloves is useful for hauling aboard boisterous species such as tope. Gloves are also the best method for rays. Only large congers still need a gaff. Never gaff a fish you intend to return alive.

Some means of removing the hook from mean-mouthed fish is useful. The Hookout is the best device, but is very difficult to find in the shops. A large pair of strong gripping pliers is a substitute.

A wooden mallet or suitable club is needed for the humane killing of any fish you want to keep. If you are in your own boat a small plastic fish box will keep the catch tidy. Some charter boats have boxes available, but they are often communal ones. Better to take your own strong sack.

A piece of flat board for cutting up bait may be supplied by the skipper, but a piece of scrap plywood of your own is useful. Certainly you would want a cutting board in your own boat.

Mackerel feathers for catching fresh bait are essential, since you never can tell when a shoal will suddenly appear. A box with a small selection of spinners, lures, attractors, muppets, Twister eels and the like is also useful.

Spare traces and miscellaneous booms, including a couple of wire ones for any sharp-toothed fish that appear, will save you having to begin making up tackle on a rolling deck, but always carry some spare line with you for tying up hooks and for any emergency when you may run out of reel line.

A reel repair emergency kit is also useful and need consist of nothing more than a small screwdriver, a pair of pliers and a roll of vinyl tape.

20 Terminal Tackle

I am a great believer in simple rigs in boat fishing. Complicated ones with lots of branch lines, excessive ironwork and multiple hooks don't seem to catch any more fish and when they tangle, boy, do they tangle!

To tie the basic terminal rigs I shall outline all you need is a modest selection of swivels, hooks, booms, beads, spare line, and the ability to tie a couple of knots. There are much more involved types of rig, but they are specialist, and really outside the confines of this book. You will also find that some rigs that go under different names are really only variations on a theme. After all, it is difficult to come up with many unique ideas for tying a hook and a weight to a line.

A rig is the same as a trace in that it is an angling expression for the arrangement of line and hook at the very end of the tackle. The hooklength (occasionally called a snood) is the length of line that attaches the hook to the main line.

Freelining

This is the simplest rig there is. Use a tucked half-blood knot to tie a hook on the end of the reel line, put some bait on and lower it over the side. Amusingly simple, it has its uses in slow-moving, shallowish water where the fish are cruising between mid-water and the surface. Being in free fall, the bait is particularly attractive to fish and the takes are often bold lunges that are unmistakable. It can be a good technique for pollack; just lower a piece of fish or a live eel into the water. You could freeline a large ragworm just hooked through the head or big lump of crab to search for a prowling bass, and it is a fun way of catching mackerel.

It is important that the tackle is very light, particularly the line; the natural springiness of the coils of line must not restrict the passage of the line through the rod rings or make the bait behave in an unnatural manner. I would suggest line of 8–12lb, a light spinning rod and a fixed-spool reel. The hook can be chosen to suit the size of bait you plan to use – say, a 1/0 for a small piece of fish or ragworm, a 3/0 for a decent-sized piece of fish and a 6/0 Aberdeen if you are tying on huge lumps of peeler crab.

A variation is to add a little weight to aid the sinking of the line, and the simplest way of doing this is to squeeze on a few large split shot or use a spiral lead fixed two or three feet above the hook. A spiral lead is cigar-shaped, with a spiral groove winding around it and a tight spiral of wire at either end. To fix it, coil the line around the top of the wire, then around the spiral groove in the body and finally round the bottom spiral of wire. The lead will now be fixed in place but, with no knots involved, it can be removed very quickly. The spiral lead need only be a few grams, as anything of substance will destroy the free-fall effect of the floating bait and, since the lead sinks first with the bait trailing behind, heavier weights encourage tangles.

One of the most deadly forms of free-lining is with a live sandeel. Hook the

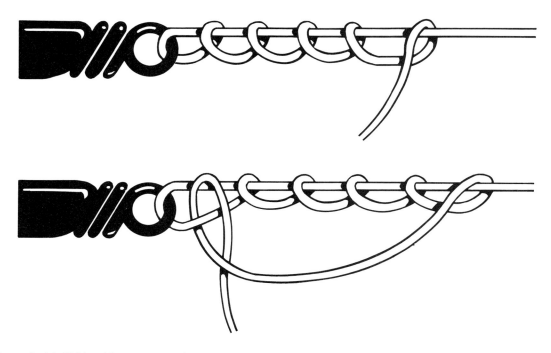

The tucked half-blood knot − use it for attaching line to hooks and swivels.

sandeel either through the top lip alone or first through the top lip and then lightly through the back. Pollack, bass, coalfish and even mackerel will leap at an eel presented in this manner.

One Hook Flowing Trace

This is the trace most commonly used in boats. Use a weight link-clip, such as the red plastic Zip slider, Kilmore, Ashpole, Sharpe tube booms or one of the other sinker clips. Slide the clip up the main line and attach a swivel to the end of the line using a tucked half-blood knot so the slider is unable to fall off the end of the line. Then tie the hook to a length of line and tie this hooklength to the swivel. Attach the sinker to the sliding clip and you have tied the second-simplest terminal rig.

The length of the hooklength is governed by several factors, mostly to do with the preference of the fish, The shorter the hooklength, the sooner the bite will be registered, the sooner the fish will feel the resistance of the sinker, and − possibly − the sooner it will spit out the hook. Short hooklengths tangle a lot less than long ones.

I would not recommend a hooklength less than 12 inches. A longish length allows the fish to pick the bait up, mouth it and possibly take it fully inside the mouth before moving off sufficiently to register the fact on the rod tip. A good average length is 3 feet. Some species respond to a bait that has some movement in it, caused by the hooklength drifting about in the current. The longer the hooklength and the greater the flow, the more likely this is to happen. You can increase this movement by tying the hooklength in thick nylon, say 35lb BS which, while grossly overgunned for the fish, moves the bait more because the

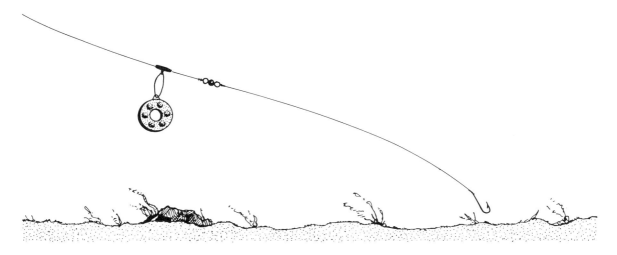

The simple one hook flowing trace – basis of so many variations.

tide affects it more than a thinner line.

Fish that respond to movement are most flatfish – particularly plaice – rays, and sometimes cod. It would not be unusual to use a hooklength as long as 6 feet for plaice fishing, and I have seen them as long as 12 feet. Traces as long as this may have some attraction for fish but they are the devil of a job to cope with for the user, since the hook is still underneath the water when the sinker bumps against the top eye of the rod. You have to handline in the last few feet of trace in order to grasp the hooklength near enough the hook to pull the fish inboard. Tiresome it may be, but very effective on occasions.

If you were to spend the whole of your boat-fishing life using only the one-hook trace you would not want for much in the way of species.

Two Hook Flowing Trace

This is a popular variation on the one hook flowing trace. As well as the main hook, a second hook is attached to the hooklength on a very short piece of nylon – only 2 or 3 inches long. This allows the presentation of two different baits and, as a bonus, the chance to catch two fish at once. The simplest way to attach the second line is by a knot called the blood loop, which is illustrated.

It is important to tie the hooklength away from the sinker, otherwise the trace may tangle during casting. I like it to be two-thirds of the way down the hooklength from the sinker. Disobey this advice at your peril . . . Do not use any kind of boom in attaching the secondary hook: booms only work when there is tension in the line.

The second hook can be of the same size and carry the same bait as the primary hook, but often it is a useful tester for an alternative bait and species. For example, while fishing for rays with fish strip you could use it to see if any worm-eating species such as plaice or cod are about.

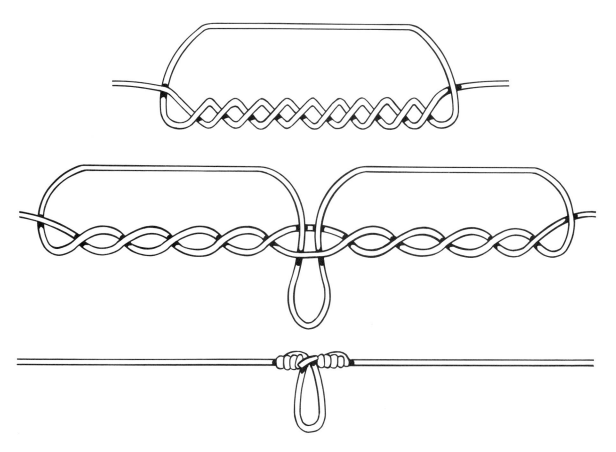

The three stages of the blood loop knot, used for putting a loop in the middle
of a piece of line.

Pennell Rig

The Pennell rig – named after the man who
invented it many years ago – uses two
hooks but only one bait. It is also called a
double-hook rig. The reason for having
two hooks in one bait is to overcome the
problem of a very big bait being taken by a
fish at the end opposite the hook. With a
hook at either end you increase (though not
double) the chance of hooking the fish. The
Pennell rig works particularly well with
very big worm baits – with five or six
inches of lug threaded up a single hook and
along the trace there is every possibility that

the bait might be seized (and a bite indication given) at some distance from the
hookpoint.

There are a number of ways of attaching
the second hook; I will give two simple
ones. Strip the three (or two) inner cables
from a short length of household electrical
cable and pull the wire out of them in short
pieces so that you have a collection of thin
plastic tubes. Cut them into ¼-inch
lengths. Tie the main hook to one end of the
hooklength and thread one of the little
plastic sleeves onto the nylon. Push the
second hook through the sleeve point first
and round the bend. Thread the line

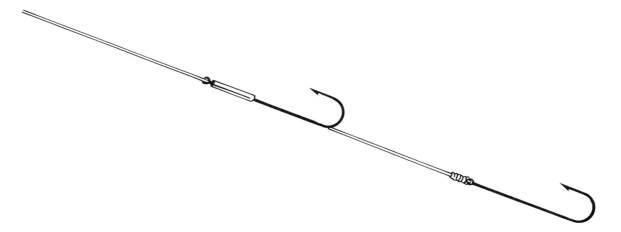

The two-hook Pennell rig, ideal for presenting very big worm and fish baits.

through the eye of the hook and tie it to swivel at the end of the main line. Both hooks should be facing the same way.

The secondary hook may be smaller than the main one, though I see no reason for it to be much smaller and I often use two of the same size. The second hook is gripped quite tightly by the plastic sleeve but with a bit of pushing you can slide it up and down the hooklength to meet the top of the bait. Bait up by threading on as much worm as you wish, then slide the second hook down the trace and push it through the top of the bait. A bonus with this rig is that the two hooks will keep frozen black lug, which is very sloppy when defrosted, neatly spread out so that it does not collapse in a huge blob around the hook bend.

If you have difficulty threading the second hook through the plastic sleeve (because you have a large hook, or a small hook and thick line), then there is a second method which I claim to be the inventor of. Thread the hooklength through the eye of the second hook and fix it in position by firmly wrapping a little piece of fabric Elastoplast tape round the shank and the hooklength. But for cutting my hand while

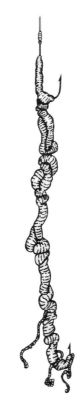

How a huge lugworm bait is presented on a Pennell rig.

fishing once, I would never have thought of that.

The double-hook rig can also be used very effectively with strips of fish, sandeel or squid and particularly live or dead whole fish baits.

Boom Trailer

This is a great rig for drift fishing with a single hook for species such as cod and whiting which tend to fly at a moving bait. A boom of your choice is connected to the line 18 inches above the sinker. The hooklength is set a few inches longer than the distance between boom and sinker so that as you drift and the tackle is pulled along the sea bed the baited hook trips the bottom in a tantalising manner.

With the boom there is very little chance of the hooklength tangling around the main line, which can happen easily when drifting with all-nylon traces. Having the boom over-depth also compensates for any variation in the sea bed, so that the bait is always hard on the bottom. You can adjust the hooklength so that it trails along the bottom by a foot or more, which will attract flatfish very well; this can only be done on clean ground or the tackle will foul on obstacles as it is dragged along.

This is the rig I used to win the individual title in the European Cod Championships, held in the Firth of Clyde, when I took a cod every three minutes for six hours.

Paternoster Rig

The paternoster, another very popular arrangement, differs from the rigs described above in that all the hooks are positioned above the sinker. The hooks branch off

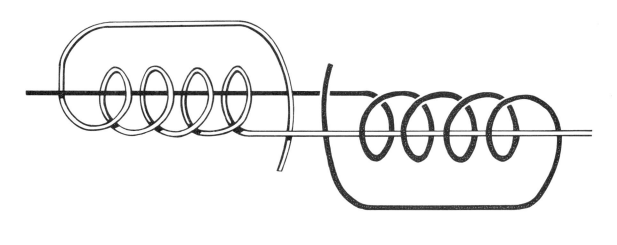

The full blood knot, used for tying two lengths of nylon line together.

rather like a set of mackerel feathers. You can tie the hooklengths direct to blood loops, in which case it would be an all-nylon paternoster, or you can use some type of standing-off boom. The all-nylon snoods are prone to twisting up so that the hooklength becomes a little more than a bump on the main line, so I always prefer a boom rig.

Do not make the hooklength much longer than the boom itself, or it will tend to tangle around the main line. There are long booms and short booms and you take your choice. Avis booms are my favourite of the short booms.

The trace is made up in advance in the following manner. You need some of the ½-inch plastic tubes used in the Pennell rig described above, a length of strongish nylon, (say 25lb BS), some superglue, a swivel with a snap link on it, an ordinary swivel and two or three booms of the type and length you prefer. The length of the nylon should be no more than 3 feet. Tie the plain swivel to one end of it and then slide on, in this order, a sleeve of plastic, a boom, two sleeves of plastic, a boom, one sleeve of plastic. Then tie the link swivel to the other end. The plastic sleeves, held in place by superglue, pinion the booms on either side. The first boom gets pushed snug up to the top swivel and the other two are spaced out evenly. Leave a fraction of space around the boom so that it may spin round freely.

This system works with free-swinging booms such as the Avis, or the popular twisted wire booms. Do not allow the top two hooklengths to overlap in length, which can cause tangling. It does not matter if the bottom hooklength trails on the sea bed, and in fact it may be desirable.

This type of rig is associated with fish that often feed slightly off the bottom, such as whiting, small codling, dogfish and coalfish. If the rig is cast away from the boat, it is extremely unlikely that any of the hooks will be off the bottom. The only effective way to keep the baits off the bottom is to fish straight up and down over the side of the boat.

The one-up one-down rig is the name I give to a hybrid between the paternoster and the one hook rig. A normal one hook rig with the hooklength trailing behind the sinker is complemented by a hook on a boom pinned above the sinker. This is a very good rig for fishing straight up and down for cod. With this rig I prefer a French boom or its near neighbour the L-boom as they can be quickly attached and adjusted up the main reel line to offer the one-up bait either almost on the bottom or several inches clear of it.

I cannot let the paternoster discussion pass by without a word on the steel spreader paternoster. Much maligned as useless ironmongery, it has a place. The two-boom steel spreader is a very efficient way of presenting two very large cod baits side by side and also a very efficient snatching rig for small flatties, whiting and pouting. Many a prominent boat angler carries one with him, although he might not admit publicly to his success with it. As with other booms, do not allow the two hooks to meet, with the risk of tangling.

Float Fishing

Conditions seldom allow float-fishing, but it is great fun. There are really only two float rigs: the fixed-depth rig and the sliding float. The slider is used where the depth is greater than the length of the rod – which is most times. Fixed-float fishing is for shallow-feeding species such as pollack, bass, mackerel and garfish, when those species choose to feed in shallow water.

There is little to explain about rigging a float for fixed-depth fishing other than to say that the line is pinned to the float by a

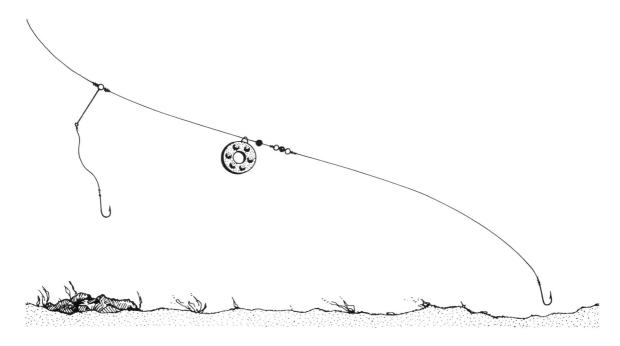

The one-up one-down rig – a useful catcher of many species.

pair of rubber rings and the float is cocked split shot squeezed on the line beneath it.

For this type of fishing the very heaviest of river floats are used. Your float needs to be long, so that the tip rides above any wavelets, and it must be highly visible. You could look at your local tackle shop's range of pike floats as one option, although these often tend to be too short.

The sliding float is a bit more involved. Again, since there are no good purpose-made sea floats, you will have to look at the range of floats designed for freshwater fishing. To rig up a sliding float, pass the line through the two small wire eyelets on the side of the float and tie on the hook. Squeeze on as much shot as you think will be needed to make the float sit up in the water. Of course, it will not cock – the weight will sink quickly to the bottom, pulling line through the float and leaving it lying on the surface. To make the float feel

the weight of the shotting, a stopping aid is put in the line at the depth at which you want the bait to be positioned. When the stopper reaches the tiny eyes on the side of the float, it cannot pass through, so the float takes up the weight of the shot and is pulled into an upright position.

The stopping device is simple, a tiny piece of line tied on the reel line with loose ends protruding from the knot. There is a proper knot called the stopper knot, but a series of simple overhand knots in a light piece of line, with the loose ends, serves perfectly well. A very easy and effective stop knot can be tied with a piece of rubber band, which doesn't unravel itself as quickly as nylon.

Because the stop knot won't tighten up properly on the main line, you can slide it up and down to adjust the depth at which the bait is held. The depth depends entirely on the whim of the fish, but one-third to

Keeping terminal rigs simple is often the most efficient way of getting fish.

Plaice can be caught on float fishing tackle where there is little depth or tidal flow.

halfway down is a good starting base. If the stop knot tends to jam in the eye of the float, thread a small drilled bead on the line between the top of the float and the stop knot.

Do not overlook the possibility of float fishing on the bottom for species such as flatfish, small codling and whiting. I have done this on a number of occasions when the tidal flow has been very slow and the depth not too great. The float puts move-ment in the bait as it is dragged along by the breeze or what tiny bit of current there is. It is not a highly productive method of fishing but it is fun. Dabs give the strangest of bites on a float.

Rubber Eel Flying-Collar Rig

This is a traditional way of fishing a soft rubber eel such as the Red Gill or Eddystone Eel. It was developed in Devon and Cornwall to take pollack and coalfish from wrecks, but has been found to catch a wide variety of fish over very differing ground.

The sinker is attached to the corner of an L-shaped wire boom, the reel line to the upward arm and the hooklength to the outward arm. The sinker will not move up and down as with the single-hook sliding trace, but is locked in place.

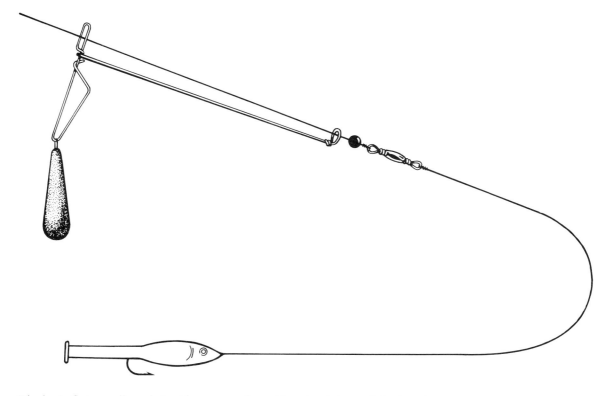

The basic flying-collar eel rig. The means of attaching the sinker and the length of line the eel is attached to are very variable.

The hooklength is very long, usually 12 feet but as much as 18 feet – some pollack specialists advocate a length of 24 feet. To the end of this elongated hooklength is tied the rubber eel. The handling of such a long hooklength is difficult and casting is impossible. The tackle is lowered over the side of the boat and allowed to stream away in the tide as it sinks to the bottom.

With such a long trace, tangling would be highly likely without the advantage of the long boom to which the hooklength is attached. This helps to separate the hooklength from the main line during the descent. The risk of tangling is also greatly decreased when there is a tide flowing as the eel is carried off in the current while the sinker makes an almost vertical descent.

The method of fishing this rig is very important. When you feel the sinker touch bottom, engage the reel spool and very slowly begin to wind the line in. A slow, steady retrieve makes the eels wobble tantalisingly in the current while they move slowly upwards. A fast retrieve would just drag the eel through the water in a most unnatural manner. You can give an occasional quick burst on the reel to make the eel dart, but soft and even is the key. When the eel has been brought up forty or fifty turns let it drop back down and start at the bottom again, but bring it right to the surface every now and then to check that the fish have not risen very high.

It is vital that the reel clutch be set very light as the fish will hit the lure very hard

When working rubber eels on a flying collar keep on reeling after the take and avoid early strikes.

and dive for the bottom, tearing off line. When this happens do not strike but continue the same steady reeling. The diving fish will have set the hook itself and all you need to do is maintain steady pressure and it will begin to rise. When the fish is near the surface, the sinker and boom will come to the rod tip before the fish has come up so you have to grab the hooklength and draw the fish towards you for netting.

Whilst this rig was designed for the rubber eel, it can also be used with a large ragworm. These worms are taken naturally in a free-swimming situation and fish readily go for one fished in the flying-collar fashion. Slivers of mackerel, squid or live sandeel can be used in the same way.

Attractors

By attractors I mean beads, spoons, spinners, silver paper and anything else that is put on a baited hook to increase its effectiveness. This is a subject that is fiercely argued over amongst all anglers, not only boat anglers. There are those who declare passionately that a spoon or string of beads is an aid to catching. The argument is that the brightness of such devices arouses curiosity in a fish, which then proceeds to swim up to investigate what is causing the unusual sight. When it arrives, it sees or smells the baited hook and attacks it. The theory is sound but has never been convincingly proved. Consequently the effectiveness of attractors continues to be a matter of individual prejudice.

Pirks can sometimes account for the unusual, such as this ballan wrasse caught while cod fishing.

I am not a regular attractor enthusiast but I have friends who are exceptionally talented boat anglers who say that they have their uses, and I would not challenge their beliefs. There are occasions when I use an attractor, but it is questionable whether the lure is the prime trap or the bait.

The most common situation is pirking over a wreck, where cod and ling are the target species. If you want to catch ling then a chunk of mackerel on the hook will invariably increase your chances, while the plain pirk will mainly catch cod.

Baited feathers are another much-used method of combining two established fish-catchers, but who can say if it is the feathers or the bait (or a combination) that is doing the damage?

All I can say is that an attractor positioned

above the bait, or a baited attractor, has accounted for a lot of fish over the years. Perhaps that is ducking the issue, but it's all you are getting from me on the matter . . .

Hooklength Material

It is a mistake to fish with hooks tied to very light line, even if the main line itself is very light. Light hooklengths bring all manner of problems. Fish with teeth will crunch straight through it, and even those which possess less effective dentition will eventually chew through light line.

I see no reason to use line of less than 12lb for hooklengths; I usually use a minimum of 15lb and often go much higher. If the fish have powerful jaws (rays, for example) or very rough skin (dogs) 28lb or 35lb is not unreasonable. I use 35lb hooklengths for large cod, ling, huss – anything that has a chance of biting through thin line.

For species which possess proper teeth – such as tope, spurs and conger – either wire or very heavy nylon is needed. For conger this heavy-duty piece need be only a foot, jointed by a strong swivel to a length of 50lb nylon to make up a hook-length of 2 feet, which is a suitable length for conger.

For tope something special is needed. Not only can tope chew through the wire, but the sandpapery flanks of the fish can abrade through line. I use 5 feet of 75lb wire, then a swivel and a further 5 feet of 75lb nylon to complete the hooklength. This trace has yet to be bitten or chafed through by a tope. Apart from the rigs described in this chapter you will see a myriad others. Every locality has its own particular favourite but a lot of them are just variations on the basic rigs I have explained.

When charter-boat fishing it is a useful exercise to ask the skipper what terminal rig works best on the grounds he is taking you

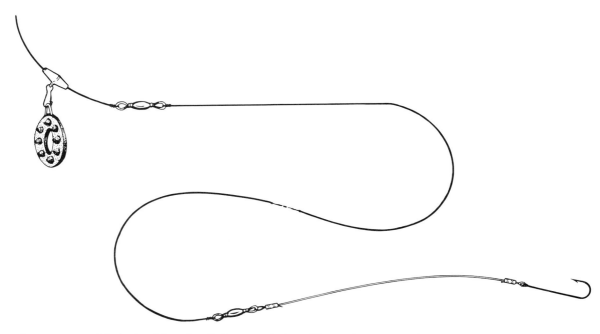

A tope trace, with the hooklength split into two halves. The section nearest the hook is 5 feet of 75lb BS trace wire, the other part 5 feet of 75lb BS nylon.

to. The skipper will be flattered that you appear to want his advice, and even if after hearing it you prefer to use your own favourite rig you have at least given yourself an opportunity to learn something new about terminal tackle. Some charter-boat skippers will suggest things that your experience tells you are unsound, but most have opinions on the best rigs based on what they have seen produce fish on their boat over the seasons. What they suggest is certainly worth a try.

21 Bait

This is not a bait book, so I shall not commit large slabs of type to digging lugworm, rummaging under weeds for crabs, and the like. What I will do is give some suggestions on the types of bait that work in a boat, how to look after bait while afloat and how to collect a little while at anchor.

The first thing to remember is that the acceptability of bait is very much a regional thing. A bait that works in one part of the country will not work in another. Explanations for this curious phenomenon are many, but probably it is related to the natural availability of the bait. The classic illustration of this is squid, a prime cod bait in the waters along the south coast yet next door to useless in northern waters.

Worm baits are used universally by boat anglers. Ordinary blow lug will catch a wide variety of fish. Black lug is that bit tougher and the large gutted black lug is very resilient. Ragworm is also excellent, and which of the two is better is often a question of regional variation.

Sunlight and warmth are the killers for worms, particularly blow lugworm, and you should make every effort to keep the bait cool and dark. A cool box is the best container. Do not allow the worms to lie on top of each other in a tub as the pressure will rapidly kill them. Similarly, if the worms are wrapped in newspaper, do not allow the paper to become wet as this will create pressure on the worms and crush them. Dry newspaper is best for keeping lugworms in good shape at sea.

Mackerel is another widely-taken bait. It catches the dog family, from irritating lesser-spotties up to tope. Conger love it, nearly all the rays do, and whiting tear enthusiastically at it. In general terms, mackerel is unsuccessful with the smaller flatfish; only turbot go for it regularly. Very large cod may take it, but smaller ones won't. Pollack will take it, coalfish occasionally. The freshness of mackerel has a direct relationship with the amount of fish it will catch. Hours matter with mackerel bait. The very complex oils soon begin to change after death and the change is accelerated alarmingly if dead mackerel is exposed to sunlight and becomes warm.

What is a very effective bait straight from the sea, one which will attract fish from far and wide, becomes progressively less efficient as the hours tick by. However, I rate carefully-kept fresh mackerel in front of frozen mackerel. After it has been frozen, the mackerel takes on a different look and texture. The flesh is firm and resilient when very fresh, but when frozen and thawed it breaks into sloppy flakes and just hangs limply on the hook. There are times when there is no choice but to use frozen, since catching mackerel while you are at sea is often difficult.

Try buying good-quality fresh mackerel from the fishmonger before you go out, and make a point of examining the mackerel on the slab before you buy it; often it will have been frozen. Thawed mackerel is given away by a dull grey look to the flesh, almost as if it had been given a coat of half-gloss varnish. The eye is similarly grey-looking. If you ask the fishmonger if the mackerel is fresh or frozen, he may well be honest with you, since fishmongers have an uncanny knack of recognising anglers who are buying fish for bait.

If you take mackerel with you in a boat in anything but chilly conditions you will be well advised to carry it in a cool-box with ice packs in. This may seem over-fussy, but I cannot emphasise how important it is to keep mackerel as fresh as possible and away from its enemy, heat.

If you are catching your mackerel at sea, put them in a spot shielded from direct light, cover them with a wet sack, and let air circulate around them – *never* keep them in a plastic bag in warm weather. Catching mackerel at sea is a matter of searching the different levels of water with feathers or other mackerel lures (Daylite lures are very good) in a likely part of the ocean.

Wise and regular boat anglers collect their own supply of mackerel for freezing on the days when they are plentiful for the days when they are not. It goes without saying that mackerel for freezing is kept as cool as possible and must hit the icicles as soon as possible after capture. Gutted whole mackerel are easy to freeze, but fillets are more compact and convenient when you come to thawing and using the bait.

Sandeels are a very good boat bait, particularly suited to inshore dinghy work. Live sandeel reigns supreme. To keep it alive at sea you need a biggish plastic bucket and a battery-powered aerator. Change the water a few times during the day and keep the aerator bubbling through an airstone. The water must not get warm and, since eels need a lot of oxygen in the water, do not overload your tank.

If you are using frozen sandeels, and the Ammo eels are excellent, then keep them as cool as possible, preferably frozen in a cool-

Peeler crab is a useful bait inshore, but not in deep water.

Livebaiting is a good method for tope, conger, cod and several other species. To keep livebaits alive, have a net tied over the top of a bucket and hang it over the side.

box until twenty minutes before you want to use them. Eels are like mackerel in that they have a very high oil content which affects both the scent and the texture of the flesh when they get warm.

Squid is often a good bait on its own, but remember my comments on its regional appeal. Calamaris are frozen and imported little squids that can be offered whole for conger or tope. A very thin trailing strip can be worked on a flying collar rig, or a small piece can be used to tip a worm bait. It is a good stand-by bait for whiting and a useful bait to have in the freezer.

Peeler crab is not the universal bait afloat that it is on shore. For cod it will work well close inshore, where the crabs are naturally found, but offshore it can fare poorly against other baits. Exceptions are smooth hounds, which respond very well to crab, and some species of rays.

Shellfish is an underrated bait. Mussel is a good bait for small-to-medium-sized cod; bunches of cockles will take flatfish; and razorfish is a very good cod bait in winter. Shellfish is not a mainstream bait but one which is always worth bearing in mind. It freezes well, too.

Livebaiting is not done much at sea, but for species such as tope, occasional big cod and other big fish it is well worth trying. Catching little pouting for bait is not that difficult but keeping them alive is. You need a very large plastic bucket and a circular piece of netting with an elasticated edge so that it can be pulled over the top of the bucket and will hold firmly in place. Lower the bucket beneath the surface of the water by means of a rope attached to the handle. The fish cannot escape because of the elasticated net and the water will be kept fresh and cool. Don't forget to retrieve the bucket when under power and when a good fish is being played into the side of the boat.

22 Keeping Warm and Dry

It is a cause of wonder to me that so many anglers spend enormous amounts of money on their tackle – even two thousand pounds on a boat and engine – and then go to the nearest outdoor discount store for their protective clothing and spend the least possible.

The sea is a hostile environment in terms of weather. I cannot recall the weather at sea ever being warmer than on land. The reverse is frequently true by many degrees. Strolling around in T-shirt and shorts is very pleasant on the quayside in summer, but once at sea it can feel like winter again. You must make sure you have adequate warm clothing and adequate dry clothing. It is in the period from spring to autumn that most anglers get caught out by the chilliness of weather at sea. In winter we all are kitted out to protect the body against the cold, but come the first rays of the warm sun and anglers are apt to forget what it is like to shiver.

A good set of waterproof trousers, jacket and hat or hood must be on board with you at all times. Even if it is a lightweight suit, there will come a time when you are thankful of having it. A pair of long trousers and a pullover are always needed in summer. You can always take a carrier bag with deck pumps, T-shirt and shorts if you like the idea and change if the sun beats down. A tub of sun cream and an eye-shade or sunglasses are also useful things to have stowed away in your box if the weather forecast promises hot sun. A huge bottle of pop will also be welcome.

When it comes to winter clothing I do not stint in quality and quantity. Buy the best you can afford. Mountaineering and skiing shops sell excellent outdoor wear. The clothing used for offshore sailing is also of excellent quality. If the sea looks anything like capable of jumping over the side of the boat once you are under way put full waterproof clothing on or move somewhere where there is total protection. While the air temperature may not dictate heavy protective clothing, should you catch a wave bouncing over the side and get drenched you will quickly lose body heat and any enthusiasm at all for carrying on fishing. It is no good waiting until the wave has hit you – protect yourself.

When selecting outer garments, remember that the description 'waterproof' is quite distinct from 'made from waterproof material'. A waterproof jacket must not let water in anywhere. Clothing made from waterproof material may well leak at the seams, since only the fabric and not the garment is being described as waterproof.

I shall disrobe and explain what and why I wear to combat the weather.

Next to my skin I have a one-piece thermal suit. Separate leggings and vest are a bit more versatile, but they can leave a gap around the middle and the bottom of the back, where cold can penetrate. I bought the best I could afford from a skiing and mountaineering shop.

My socks are calf-length ski socks, knitted in a very thick weave. A second pair of cheap long socks over the top will prevent the ski socks from chafing on the inside of the boot.

My trousers are from an old suit, with a high wool content. Denim jeans are cold. I have a high-quality lumberjack shirt, also bought from a mountaineering shop, and my wife knits me a new jumper every ten years from heavy-duty wool.

Moon boots are essential. They are impractical for beach launching if you have your own boat because of their shortness, but after waders have been used for this purpose, a change of footwear can be made in the boat. For charter-boat fishing you can put on your moon boots as soon as you are ready to embark. Waders are very cold and cramp the knee joints when you are sitting down. Moon boots with waterproof bib-and-brace trousers over the top are unbeatable for winter.

My jacket (which I take with me winter and summer) is a Henri-Loyd Glencoe jacket and it is marvellous. I have a flotation lining in it for safety and it is totally waterproof. I have two pairs of bib-and-brace overtrousers – one heavyweight for winter, one lightweight for summer. Never get elasticated-waist waterproofs – they just gradually drift down to hang at half-mast around your backside.

I have two pairs of gloves. One pair are waterproof ski-mitts, which I take off only for baiting up and tying knots. The other pair are long industrial rubber gloves; they are used for wet jobs such as gutting fish or hauling the anchor.

I have a good-quality balaclava, a good wool scarf and the hood from my jacket. This clothing is not excessively bulky and I seldom get really cold. Such attention to quality is important in a small boat because, unlike the charter boat, there is no room to walk about to keep the circulation moving.

Charcoal-burning handwarmers are a clever little aid to warming fingers, though sometimes troublesome to keep alight. flasks of hot drinks and soup are common sense; tots of rum are not. Alcohol is nice and cheery, but it leads to a lowering of the resistance to bad weather, both mentally and physically. What a shame . . .

BOAT-FISHING TECHNIQUES

23   Fish Location

It might be thought that the question of fish location concerns only the dinghy angler and not the man in the charter boat. This is not so. Fish location is just as important to the angler in the charter boat as to the one in the dinghy. The similarity is greatest when it comes to locating fish within the immediate area of where the boat has been positioned, when some fine adjustment is still required of the angler to put the bait in front of the fish. For this reason I think that the charter-boat angler will find much of interest in this chapter. If it does nothing else it will help the angler to interpret what the skipper is doing.

The ability to find fish is one of the really important skills of the angler who fishes from his own boat. Hooks, lines and even bait play a marginal role in success compared to fish location: where you drop your anchor is the most important decision of the day.

Your greatest aid in locating fish is your own experience and the experience of others. A close second is a notebook in which you log in your experiences. This need not be done on a grand scale; it might take the form of jottings alongside the tide table for a given year. In a vague sort of way you may know that plaice show in late spring in Sandy Bay. If you pencil in the first date when you – or anyone – get a good catch, you have a note not only of the date but also of the tidal conditions. I am not suggesting that you become a professional diarist, or that you give chapter and verse on every trip, but if something happens that is outside the norm having a

permanent record will prove invaluable in later years.

The next problem is your exact location when you make a notable catch. Unlike a beach, where there are innumerable identifying features almost underfoot, at sea the water is remarkably uniform. You can take compass bearings on landmarks, but such fine points of coastal navigation are not really the meat and drink of anglers. Neither can you accurately guess what distance offshore you are.

It is usually possible to reposition yourself by eye over a wide area of a particular ground that is known to hold fish, but smaller areas present real problems. The simplest answer is to make use of navigational buoys if they are around. A timed course from an outer buoy can be quite accurate, and this method is used by a lot of charter-boat skippers. Make a note of times and courses from any prominent buoys and keep the list safe on board. Not only will it be useful for locating fish; it will also point the way home should visibility deteriorate.

A second method is to have a note of the alignment of objects on the shore. A chimney stack just disappearing over a hill, the harbour lighthouse in front of the bus station, anything like that can help. Using landmarks such as yellow cornfields is not recommended, due to the harvesting habits of farmers . . .

Another way of picking out a mark is to co-ordinate the throttle setting, the compass bearing and your watch. If it takes ten minutes at half-throttle on a south-west setting to reach a favourite mark on one

Getting right on top of a wreck can result in all anglers on board into fish at
the same time.

day, it will be similar on another. Tidal flow
and a slight difference in throttle setting
might throw the positioning off, but this is
another tool to use.

The job becomes a lot easier if you have a
sounder on board, even a simple red
blipper. A set that gives you just the bare
depth enables you to correlate the landmarks with the depth of water you expect
to be fishing in. The simple sounder will
show up things such as troughs and banks,
submerged rivers and, in a very rough way,
whether the sea bed is very rocky or
smooth. Despite claims to the contrary,
these very basic sounders do not show fish
clearly. For that you need a more sophisticated sounder, one that shows a full
segment of the sea bed in graph-form –

either a paper sounder, which I prefer, or a
video type, which a lot of other anglers
prefer. The individual merits of each type
are discussed in Chapter 7. While the two
types of sounder present information in
slightly different forms, the information
itself is the same and the following comments apply to both.

The instruction book that comes with
your sounder will give you details on how
to interpret the screen image. The picture is
not a crystal-clear image of fish and rocks in
perfect profile. Instead, the bottom shows
up as a dark wedge, and it is the clarity and
shape of the top of this wedge that indicates
the nature of the sea bed. If the profile is
smooth and even, that is the nature of the
sea bed. Experience will help you determine

If you have not got an electronic navigator, writing down an alignment of marks on the shore will give an approximate guide to where you are.

what is sand and what is mud. A stony sea bed will show up as slightly zigzag and very rocky ground will look decidedly zigzag.

Fish are picked up by the sounder when this signal is reflected by the air in the fishes'

swim bladders. Since most forms of flatfish have no swim bladder (apart from the fact they hug the bottom) it is almost impossible to pick up this type of fish. Fortunately, cod have huge swim bladders so they are very

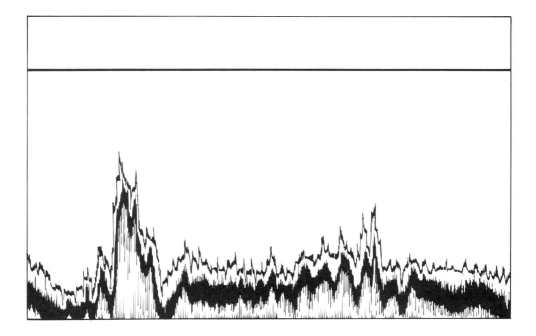

The surface may be flat, but an echo sounder can pick up fish-holding pinnacles below. The lower picture shows what is actually present, the upper picture is how that image is presented on the paper-fed echo sounder.

easy to pick up. Fish are marked on the graph by a scratch mark; a tight shoal of fish will show as a close-knit group of scratches. There are pitfalls, though. A shoal of white-bait will look like an enormous shoal of fish, air bubbles will sometimes appear as fish marks if the sensitivity control is incorrectly set, and even dense plankton can confuse the soundings.

A common error is to interpret a picture shown while the boat is moving at speed. This gives a very distorted view of the seabed. A fall in depth that occurs gradually over several yards will appear as an abrupt ledge and the bottom appears far more rugged than it actually is because of the stringing out of distance between signals. The most accurate picture will be recorded when the boat is moving very slowly, although this is not always practical.

Tides

A quite different skill in fish location is understanding how tide and current affect the movement and feeding habits of fish. Very few fish feed better when there is no tidal flow. Many species will take bait at the top of the tide, but catches will compare very unfavourably with when the tide is moving. Why this is so has never been wholly proven, but the cause is of less concern to anglers than the effect. The tidal flow is at its slowest around the period of turning. At big spring tides the turn is faster (and therefore there is less slack water) than on small neap tides. ('Spring' does not refer to the season of the year; it is the other meaning of the word, to leap high. Neap means low. The height of a tide is expressed in metres and measured on a gauge in the harbour for which the tide times are being quoted. A 10-metre tide means the depth of water on the gauge will show a 10-metre change from high tide to low.)

Some fish choose to feed at different states of the tidal flow, but this is often a regional variation. Cod may take freely in the first hour of the flood in Kent but prefer the last hour in Scotland. It is up to you to learn how the fish on your home beat react to different states of the tide.

On spring tides, with their greater range, a bigger volume of water must be shifted in the six hours or so of each tidal movement, so it runs much faster than on smaller tides. Since fish feed better with some movement in the water, does a spring tide automatically spell better fishing? Not always. Some fish shy away from fierce flow, some seem to feed better in it, but the greatest problem for the angler is coping with the effect of fierce flow on his tackle. Line streams away from the boat and very heavy sinkers are needed to hold bottom. Maybe you can't hold, or the fishing becomes so unpleasant you pack up or move to quieter water. Again, it is a matter of evaluating the local conditions.

It would be confusing and probably mis-leading for me to give set rules for fishing different tidal states, but I can offer some pointers. Try to plan your fishing trip around the movement of the tide rather than the convenience of nine till five. This is where the angler in his own boat can score heavily over the charter boat, which tends to work fairly rigid hours. By going out much earlier or later in the day you can get the benefit of all the productive period of the tide. It is foolish to spoil your chances by including too much slack water in your fishing time. Learn the movements of fish in your area in relation to the tides, and use that knowledge to get the best from your craft and from your time.

If you want to get the best catches it is important to study the effect of tides on the marks you fish.

Short Cuts to Fish Location

There are much more direct ways of finding good fishing than the procedures I have outlined. Look for a boat you recognise as one with a good track record and fish near it. It might be a charter boat or another private boat. This might not be cricket, but, like the high bouncer, it works. Alternatively, keep a keen ear on the VHF radio while you are at sea. Listen for conversations between other anglers, or ask outright if anybody is catching. This will only work for a short while unless you offer good information in return. Unless you do reciprocate, you will be met with silence or – worse – lies.

A little more conventional is to ask for information before you put to sea – perhaps from a tackle dealer or from someone on the quayside. You can also keep an eye on the angling press, which can sometimes offer guidelines.

24 Baiting the Hook

Do not forget the importance not only of having the best bait you can get but of keeping it in good condition during the day's fishing. This is not an encyclopedia of bait so I do not include the rarer offerings and baiting-up methods, but the information provided will enable you to deal with any bait. The baits themselves are dealt with in Chapter 21.

Lugworm

Lug is used in three forms − as a live complete animal when it is small-to-medium in size; as a dead and gutted worm when it is large; and as a frozen gutted worm. Three different hooking techniques are needed. What is common to all varieties of lugworm is that the sand tail should be nipped off with finger and thumb and discarded. There is nothing of attraction in the tail and it can be difficult to bait up.

Lugworm is often called blow lugworm because of its habit of turning to jelly, or 'blowing', when it dies. This blowing process can be held back for two or three days by keeping the worms very cool. It is speeded up to a matter of an hour or so if they are exposed to hot sun in a deep mound. In practice, try to buy or dig your lugs the day before you go fishing and keep them as cool as possible, never letting them lie on top of each other.

Hooking techniques for blow lug depend on the size of the worm and the size of the bait you wish to present, but always thread them on tail-first so that the head is the last part to be penetrated by the hook point. This will limit the loss of body fluid from the worm, even if you are threading two or more up a hook for a large cod offering. If you are after a fish with a large appetite and mouth to match, such as cod, it is best to pile on plenty of bait. I would think five inches of worm a reasonable length, and the amount of lug needed to make this offering depends on the size of the worms you have. You should reduce the amount to half that for small species such as whiting and flatfish, but always err on the generous side. While lug that have blown are difficult to thread on a hook they are still worth using since fish will still take them.

For those unfamiliar with the gutted lugworm, it is a large type of lugworm, growing as long as ten inches. When the worm is removed from the pressure of its burrow and exposed to the air the internal body pressure will, after a few minutes, force the gut of the worm through its head. This may damage the texture of the flesh, so the digger usually strikes the worm on the spade immediately after capture to kill it and force the gut out. While it may seem that the main attraction of the worm has been left behind, in fact the gutted worm has two qualities that the smaller blow lugworm has not.

The gutted worm will keep much longer if kept cool, since it cannot blow as ordinary lug can. Three or four days are quite possible if the worms are wrapped in dry newspaper and kept in a cold fridge. The only deterioration in the bait is the normal putrefaction of flesh. This is not always a bad thing and gutted worms with a slightly off hum account for some good fish. Because of the size of the gutted lug, it is possible to use them whole for large fish such as cod, or break them in two or even three pieces for whiting or flatfish. It depends on the size of the gutted worms you have and the size of the fish you are after.

If you are using small pieces, simply thread them on to the hook. Since the worm has a hollow running through the middle the hooking is a very easy process. The flesh is very firm and should you want to use a whole gutted worm just thread it up the line so that it stops at the bend of the hook. With large worms it helps to use the Pennell hook rig described in Chapter 20 so that the bait has a hook at each end. It does not matter which way round you put a gutted black lug on the hook. Because much of the water content has been taken out of the worm in the gutting process, and also because of its size, the gutted lugworm is very suitable for freezing to provide a useful stand-by bait for the times when fresh worms are not available. You may buy them already frozen or use the following method to freeze them yourself. Lay a sheet of plastic on a tin tray, place the worms to be frozen on the plastic and put all in the freezer with the blower on fast-freeze. With all the worm exposed to the chill air the freezing process is faster. When they are frozen, wrap them up in tens in sheets of newspaper and then seal them in plastic bags to prevent freezer burn. They can be transported still frozen in a large, wide-mouthed food flask and unused worms can be returned to the freezer still frozen.

Whole thawed lugworms require the Pennell rig as they go very limp and will sag in a blob if not supported by a hook at either end. The double-hooking technique is not needed if you only use small pieces.

Ragworm

Ragworm is always used live. It can be frozen but when thawed it is very soft and difficult to use. You thread a ragworm just like a lugworm. The tail tapers to a thin point so you push the hook into the body at the head and leave a bit of tail wiggling at the end. If you wish to try hooking the ragworm tail first you will have to make the point of penetration some way up from the tail to prevent the worm simply breaking up.

That is the usual way of hooking ragworm, but there is another very effective method – hooking by the head only so that the worm is allowed to wiggle tantalisingly in the tide. Take a firm hold of the ragworm's head, avoiding the nippers, and **push** an Aberdeen fine-wire hook firmly

Ragworm spread out on newspaper to dry and toughen up before they are put on the hook.

down the centre of the worm for no more than half an inch before bringing the point out. Ragworm baited this way must be cast gently but are very effective in clear water. If the rag are small two or three can be used in this manner. This is the way to bait ragworm if you wish to troll with them or fish sink-and-draw for bass or pollack.

Mackerel

Having got your mackerel – and I cannot overemphasise the importance of freshness – the only other thing you need is a board to cut it on and a sharp knife. A blade that is not sharp will tear the mackerel and make poor fillets.

If you are after shark it is a simple matter to bait up with mackerel. You push the hook through the upper jaw and cast out. If your mackerel are small or your ambitions high, you can use two small mackerel hooked together. A small mackerel can be fished in this way for tope.

For smaller baits you must cut the mackerel up. There are several ways of doing this. Place the mackerel sideways on the cutting board. Make a deep vertical cut just behind the gills until you meet the resistance of the backbone. Turn the knife parallel to the backbone and cut and slide the knife along the backbone until the blade comes out of the fish at the tail. Remove the fillet and repeat the process after reversing the mackerel. You now have three baits – the two fillets and the head, backbone and guts left behind. The head and guts are often thrown away, but can be a very useful catcher of ling and conger over a wreck. This is often the bait the skipper uses by passing his hook through the head of the carcass, hence its nickname 'skipper's fillet'.

A fillet can be hooked whole or cut up in to smaller baits. If the mackerel is very fresh its texture will be very firm. The hook can simply be passed through it a couple of times, starting at the tail end and finishing at the broad end, and no further attention is needed. A full fillet is the size of bait used for tope, conger, ling and large rays.

If the fillets are a bit old and the flesh is starting to break up you will have to pinion the fillet at the pointed end by lashing it on the line with a piece of elastic thread. Grip the line, the tail end of the mackerel and the end of the elastic cotton between finger and thumb, bind it around the bait half a dozen times or so (it is not critical), then just pull the cotton and snap it. It will not unravel as the turns will bite into the flesh of the mackerel.

To cut up smaller pieces of mackerel for catching whiting, smaller rays, dogfish and the like, place a fillet on the cutting board and make strips of a length that suits. Keep all these pieces well protected from sunlight and heat as they will deteriorate very quickly.

There is a way of preparing a small whole mackerel for tope, conger or ling which involves removal of the backbone. Lay the mackerel on the cutting board and slide the knife along the backbone from the tail to the head. Remove the knife, turn the mackerel and repeat the process. Separate the two halves and take a firm hold of the backbone, twist and pull it away. A pair of pliers or strong scissors helps. Hook the mackerel through the upper jaw.

Since mackerel is a bulky bait, guard against using too large a piece on too small a hook, with the risk of masking the hookpoint.

Squid

If you wish to try squid – and remember the regional variation in its effectiveness – it is a very easy bait to prepare. You can buy either large, fresh native squid or the smaller frozen imported calamari squid. I prefer fresh natives. Whichever you choose, prepare it by taking hold of the tentacles and pulling out the middle of the squid. It is not necessary to clean out the squid as thoroughly as a cook might; just empty it to leave a hollow pod. Cut thin strips from the body and cut up the tentacles similarly.

The size and the number of strips you use are determined by the size of the fish you are after. If you are hoping to take a big cod, conger or ling, a large hook with a whole calamari squid is not out of place. Plaice and turbot can occasionally be caught on very long, thin strips of squid fished on light tackle so that the bait rolls around in the tide. Worm baits tipped with little strips of squid are often effective for whiting.

Crabs

Peeler shore crabs are not a very good bait in offshore water where they are not found naturally. However, they can be very good for fishing close inshore or on banks and reefs. Cod, bass, flounder, rays, smooth hounds and smaller dogs will all take peelers willingly.

While the shore angler takes great care in the selection, preparation and hooking of a peeler crab, the boat angler has less need of such finesse. Pull off the legs and nippers and remove the shell by prising it off with your fingernails. If the crab is difficult to peel it is enough to remove the legs and the back shell and not bother with the under-body shell. The crab can be bound on the

Peeler crab is a super bait for big ballan wrasse like this specimen.

hook with elastic thread. Hold the crab and the end of the elastic thread against the hook and wind the thread tightly around the crab body. As the pressure builds up the crab will be burst by the thread, which allows the body fluid to seep along in the tide and attract the fish.

There is no need to peel or remove the legs of soft crabs; just bind the crab onto the hook. If the crabs are small you may need two; if they are very large you may have to cut them in half. Dead crabs have no fish appeal, so protect your bait from heat and keep it damp.

Sandeels

Sandeels make superb bait alive and are still worth using when dead and frozen. To keep sandeels alive you need a large bucket with a battery-powered aerator strapped to the side and an airstone. Do not overload the bucket, and make sure that the water is cool. Sandeels will live for a short time in a dark box full of cold, damp seaweed over a layer of frozen ice packs to keep their body temperature very low and so make them lethargic.

To hook a live sandeel pass a fine-wire Aberdeen hook through its upper jaw. Do not cast violently or the sandeel will fly off. Sandeels must be fished on light tackle so that they flutter about in the tide. Live sandeel is the bait for such species as bass and pollack which prefer a moving bait.

Turbot, rays and dogs will respond to frozen sandeels as well as to live ones. Blast-frozen sandeels are essential. The flesh is so delicate that if the freezing is done in a conventional home freezer the thawed sandeel is very pulpy and difficult to handle. Ammo brand eels are the most widely available and they are excellent quality, a couple of smaller firms also supply blast-frozen eels. Keep the sandeels frozen in a food flask or under ice-packs in a cool-box until you need them. They will defrost in sea water in a matter of minutes. When they are thoroughly thawed, bait them by passing a fine-wire Aberdeen hook through the mouth and bringing it out through the anus. You will have to thread the eel carefully around the bend of the hook to avoid bursting it.

And There's More . . .

The less widely used baits can also prove excellent fish catchers. Shellfish are a useful bait occasionally, and these are bound to the hook with elasticated cotton. Mussel and razorfish are the two commonest shellfish used as bait, though cockles are a useful bait for whiting and haddock, and scallops are a favourite in Scotland for cod and haddock.

As well as mackerel, herring is often used as a fish bait. It is a useful stand-by, often available from the fishmonger's when fresh mackerel is not. Prepare it in much the same way as mackerel, though the fish has many more bones. The smaller members of the herring family also make useful baits – a sprat is a convenient size for rays, dogfish and small conger.

How Long Does It Last?

How long baits should be left in the water depends on the type. Fish baits have a good scent trail that will last, I would guess, at least fifteen minutes. A large piece of fish bait from a freshly killed fish may last longer.

Worm baits are not so resilient, and ten minutes is as long as one can be left without some inspection. Often the period a bait is left out is governed by other factors, such as a bite, a fish, or the fouling up of the tackle on an obstruction, but the 10–15 minute rule is a good baseline.

25   Boat-Casting

It must be twelve years or more since the practice of flinging the tackle up the tide instead of merely lowering it over the side first gained publicity. It produced then, and continues to produce now, exceptionally good catches of fish in the right tidal conditions. Results from fishing down the side of the boat cannot compare with what boat-casting can achieve, yet the method still has not gained the confidence of a wide public

and for many anglers it remains a peculiarity of Essex, where it was nurtured.

I am frequently told that boat-casting is a very old technique, both in this country and on the Continent. There is an unending stream of people who were practising this method of boat fishing before charter-boat skippers Bob Cox and John Rawle from Bradwell in Essex 'invented' it in the early 1970s. Cox and Rawle have never claimed

When boat-casting, reel furiously as soon as the fish takes and pull into the fish.

to be the inventors of boat-casting, but they must take the credit for two things: bringing it to a wider audience through their articles in *Sea Angler* magazine and refining it into a successful method for catching many more species than the cod for which it was first intended. To those who claim to have known about the method before the Cox and Rawle revelations I say, flint-hearted you for not revealing your knowledge!

Boat-casting is sometimes called uptide fishing. This is a misleading name, since the practice is not to cast uptide exclusively but merely to cast away from the anchored boat. Getting away from the immediate vicinity of the boat is an advantage because of the disturbance to fish caused by the slapping motion of a boat at anchor. This thudding unsettles the fish and many, but not all, will drift away to quieter water. A second reason for the success of boat-

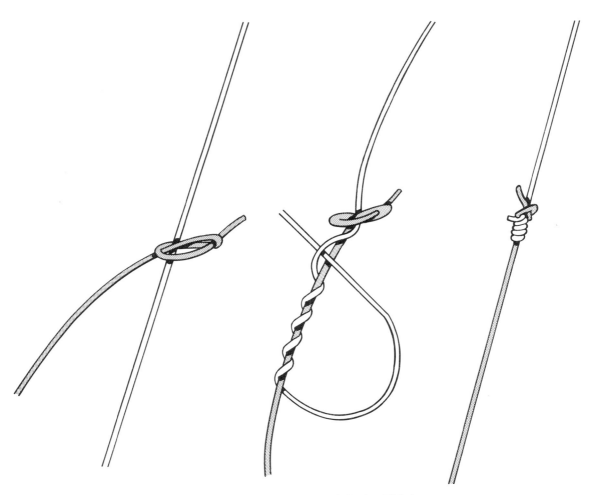

When boat-casting with light lines you will have to use a shock leader. This is the leader knot to use. The shaded line is the leader material, which should be of 35lb BS or more.

casting is the nature of the terminal tackle used, which encourages the fish to hook itself without the need for the exact timing of the strike required when fishing immediately below the boat.

Boat-casting will work in quite deep water, but is at its most effective in 50 feet or less of water and in strong tidal flow. The fish that respond to the method are cod, rays, tope, larger dogs, turbot and large plaice. It is not really a suitable method for knocking out a lot of small fish such as whiting, little codling and flatties, which can be caught in good numbers simply by dropping your tackle over the side.

In boat-casting, a wired sinker is used to hold the tackle in place. This grips fast into the sea bed and does not move. When a cod picks up the baited hook and moves off, it is stopped immediately in its tracks by the rock-solid weight; the abrupt halt, the sharp prick and the panic of the fish result in the fish pulling the hook into its mouth before the angler has picked up the rod.

That is some of the theory of boat-casting; here is the kind of tackle you will need. Since the nature of the method involves casting, the rod must be able to cast, which means length and tip speed. Full-blown beach rods are totally unmanageable in a small boat and the length should be between 8 and 10 feet; given the choice, go for 9-foot rods. The action must be fast-taper, with a soft tip and rigid middle and lower sections. You can cobble together a very good boat-casting rod by cutting down from the butt end an unwanted but sound beach rod.

The reel must also be capable of casting. The Shimano Speedmaster and Abu 7000 are two perfectly suited models, but any reel that will cast over 70 yards without trouble is suitable. Avoid small baitcasting reels as the retrieve on these is slow and you will have trouble picking up the line with a fish running towards you.

Thornback rays respond well to boat-casting. The nose grapnel sinker used here is good for very strong tides.

The line need only be 18lb BS, but you will need a casting shock leader of 35lb BS. The terminal gear can be the standard one hook rig or the Pennell two hook rig described in Chapter 20. Use a hooklength of between 2 and 3 feet.

Fixed-wire sinkers are preferable to swivel-wire ones because they cannot break free on the take of a fish and so prevent the hookpoint from ramming home. The nose-grapnel type hold the best, but as long as there are long wires the sinker will hold. You will need a selection of them, ranging from 4 to 8oz. Seldom will any more than 8oz be needed to make the wires bite into the ground and hold the tackle in position.

In a charter boat there is a fairly rigid

pattern to which each angler on board must conform so that tangles do not occur. With a couple of anglers in a boat the direction of casting is much less important. Just cast out 60 yards plus slightly away from the line of the anchor. When the sinker hits the water, check the spool, then release it to allow the line to pay out. When the sinker hits the bottom you will feel it. Continue paying out line as the tide pulls at it to form a large bow. This is one of the key points of the boat-casting method. The bow of line sinks low in the water and the current pulls on it and drives the prongs of the sinker into the sea bed. Without the bow the sinker would soon dislodge. The theory of making a boat-casting rig hold the bottom is exactly the same as making a ship's anchor hold fast.

The weight of the sinker and the amount of line you need to pay out to get it to hold cannot be learned from books, only from experience. Naturally, the stronger the tidal flow the more lead and line is needed. You will know if you have let out too little line because the sinker will not hold. If it doesn't seem to hold no matter how much line you let out then the weight of the sinker must be increased. It is all very much a matter of trial and experience.

You will see a bite very much in the ordinary way. The rod tip will rattle or it may spring back from its tensioned position as the bolting fish races away trying to shake the hook free. It is vital that you now take up the slack in the line before attempting to strike the rod. Aim the rod tip in the direction of the fish and wind as fast as you can to take up all the slack. When you feel the fish bump, arc the rod high in the sky (still reeling) and try to feel the fish. Only ease up in the retrieve when you see the rod bend over as the fish is obviously hooked.

If you are in your own boat and have the space, it makes an interesting experiment to fish one rod in the conventional manner and another in the boat-casting mode and compare results. Boat-casting does not win all the time, but it does most of the time – particularly when there are not a lot of fish about but the quality is good. Boat-casting will not beat conventional over-the-side fishing when there are a lot of small fish about, since the operation is much longer.

26 Bite Detection and Striking

If you prop your rod on the side of the boat and tighten up the line, when a fish pulls at the baited hook it will rattle the end of the rod. This is the simplest form of bite and easy to spot. Life afloat is not that simple . . .

This type of bite is easy to spot and needs no explanation, but when the sea is unsettled and the boat is moving with the swell it is not unusual for the distance between the boat and the sea bed to vary by six feet and even more. The tackle is being dumped on the sea bed then lifted several feet in the air. Not only does this play havoc with bite detection but it makes it difficult to get a fish to take the bait in the first place.

To combat this, where there is a heavy swell create as much distance between the bait and the rod tip as possible by casting away from the boat or letting the tackle be swept down the tide by the pull of the current. You can also help to reduce the effect of this swinging up and down by raising and lowering the rod tip in tune with the swells.

When a bite occurs you can pick up the rod and sweep it back in a high arc above your head, feeling for the contact with the fish. The high sweep is necessary to pick up any loose line. If this proves insufficient then you may have to try reeling in to pick up the slack line and striking at the same time.

If you really want to be on the ball in hitting bites you should hold the rod. With the shortness and lightness of boat rods this is not difficult and it will almost always result in your seeing a bite quicker and being able to respond to it quicker.

If you find that you are missing bites, try leaving them a little longer to develop. Alternatively, increase the length of the hooklength – as much as double unless you are already using a very long hooklength.

Plaice give notoriously difficult bites and can be very difficult to hook.

Just before striking, lower the rod tip so that a full arc can be used to set the hook.

This is a very good method of tackling missed bites since it allows the fish a lot more time to take in the baited hook properly before it feels the resistance of the tackle and signals the bite on the rod. If this does not work try shortening the trace down to 12 inches. When the fish picks up the bait it only has to move a short distance and the hook is pulled up abruptly, with luck to be driven home in the fish's mouth – not a very romantic way of hooking a fish but effective.

27 Artificial Lures

Tossing out a light lure on a lightweight spinning outfit is one of the great fun methods of fishing and should be tried whenever possible from either charter boat or private dinghy. The species that respond to lures are bass, pollack and coalfish, mackerel and garfish. These are the mid-water species that are quite happy to rise well clear of the bottom to take a lunge at some food.

The choice of lure is quite bewildering. There are so many available that I have little choice but to trot out those which have served me well in different parts of the country. The soft rubber eel is a universal fish catcher. The Red Gill is my favourite, but others have their own strong following. Colour of eels is something of a folklore in itself. Black has a strong following; so has red. Colour does appear to make a difference on some days, but it is impossible to draw up a regular pattern of which colour will work. I had better duck the issue and suggest carrying a range of colours till you find the one that suits your patch of ocean.

These eels have no weight in themselves, so casting weight is added in the form of an external sinker – either a slim barrel lead held in place by pinched shot or a spiral lead with the curly bits of wire at each end, which is wound on the line. Position the weight 2 feet away from the eel so as not to interfere unduly with its action. Do not use any more lead than you need to reach the ground you want to fish.

Similar to the eels in theme are the rubber worms with the floppy tails, the most popular of which are Mister Twister worms. I think the worm shape has little bearing on their ability to catch fish – they are just brightly coloured lumps of rubber with floppy tails. Some Mister Twister lures are available with lead-weighted heads so you can cast the lure on its own without additional weight.

There are several bar-type lures I like. The Ceba bar is a good catcher and the Abu Krill lure is another long-standing favourite. Abu Toby lures are universal fish takers

Bass respond well to spun lures – this 4lb fish fell to an Abu Toby.

and one of the really good bass lures I have used is the Rapala plug. Since these lures have the weight in the body, there is no need to add any lead to the tackle.

When fishing for pollack, do not use very light line for attaching the lures. This fish has a row of very tiny teeth that grind through thin line during a scrap.

The speed at which you spin the lure is not vital. By varying the speed you may, in fact, attract a fish. You do not want the lure breaking the surface, but nor should you fish it so slowly that it begins to sink to the bottom.

Pirk Fishing

Pirk fishing is fishing up and down considerably heavier lures known as pirks or jugs. For fishing over clean ground or not-too-savage reefs, where the losses are much lower than when drifting over a deep-water wreck in a charter boat, I like to use commercially made pirks. The models made by Abu really do have the edge over DIY ones; it is only their cost that prohibits their widespread use.

The range of weights you need depends on the depth and flow of the water you will be fishing in, but pirks of more than 7oz make fishing hard work over a prolonged period. Do not use a pirk any heavier than it needs to be to reach the bottom comfortably without a lot of line streaming away from the boat.

Different fish normally feed at different levels when pirking, and it is important to work your pirk accordingly. If cod are the target, the pirk must work the bottom three feet of sea and no higher. You must be able to feel the pirk hit the bottom on each lowering of the rod tip; if you can't, pay out more line until you can feel the bottom. Only when you cannot feel the bottom after paying line out, or when the line has bellied

out a long way from the boat, should you wind in and drop back down.

There is no need for a furious action when pirking. Allow the pirk to touch bottom, engage the reel and tighten up with the rod pointing down towards the water. Lift the rod tip smartly to just above the horizontal position, then lower the tip back down to feel the pirk touch the bottom again. If you heave the rod to a high vertical position there will be no way you can strike the fish properly. The fish will often be hooked during the normal pull-up action, but an extra jerk may be required.

If you are after pollack or coalfish you must search a higher level of the water. These two cousins may be taken close to the bottom but often they are several feet up, or even approaching mid-water. A sounder may pinpoint their feeding level, otherwise you just have to search with the lure. Most pirk fishing is done on the drift, which gives extra movement to the lure.

If you are pirk fishing in a charter boat in deep water, possibly over a wreck, you are going to need a heavyweight approach right through your tackle. Lures may need to be 1lb or even more to keep position in the face of strong tidal forces. You can buy lures of this weight but it is cheaper to make them. To make pirks you need 16 or 18-gauge stainless-steel wire and chromed steel tubing of a diameter not less than ½ inch and not more than 1 inch. A scrap pram offers a wealth of pirk-building materials, but a regular nosey round the municipal rubbish tip will reveal all sorts of unlikely sources.

First snip off some 3-inch lengths of the wire, bend them into a U-shape and then twist back the ends to form lugs. The lugs are very important as they will hold the wires in the pirk when they are buried by the lead. Cut a length of tubing 8 inches long and hammer one end until it is almost closed. Heat the pirk slightly to drive off

When fishing for cod it is important to concentrate on the bottom 3 feet of water, where the cod mainly feed.

any moisture in the metal, which would cause the molten lead to spit. Then put in one of the U-loops, push it almost home and hammer the flattened end of the pirk as tight shut as possible. Lock the pirk in a vice. Using gloves and goggles, pour the molten lead into the open end of the pirk. When it is near the top, with a pair of pliers

Light rods and reels, pirks and a mark close under a cliff-face: perfect conditions for pollack fishing.

Home-made pirks are much more sensible where heavy losses can be expected.

fit a second U-shape of wire into the pirk so that the bend just clears the top of the pirk. Fill the pirk with molten lead and leave it to cool.

When it is cold, weigh the pirk on kitchen scales. This will enable you to calculate what length of chrome bar you must cut to make pirks of the desired weight. Experience will tell you what weight of pirks you need for the grounds and tidal speed you fish, but seldom should you need pirks of more than 1½lb and 1lb is a good average size.

The pirk is finished off by fitting a 30mm round split ring to either end. I do not recommend oval split rings as they are

prone to breaking after constant knocking on the sea bed. You fit a hook at one end – it does not matter which. Traditionally, a large treble is used as this will foul-hook fish as well as take them in the proper manner. For a while I experimented with single hooks and found that neither the catch rate nor the proportion of foul-hooked fish seemed to alter. You will find it more convenient if you fit the hook only when you wish to use the pirk as this prevents corrosion of the hooks and prevents the pirks tangling up in the box or bucket they are kept in.

With this type of rough-and-tumble pirk fishing lines should be of 35lb BS at least; if you are fishing into heavy wrecks 50lb is

A bucket is a neat way of carrying home-made pirks about without risk of them all tangling up.

needed to avoid unacceptable losses. Again, experience will be your guide.

It is common to fit a couple of extra lures above the pirk when wreck fishing – usually the imitation-squid lures popularly called 'muppets'. For cod fishing these should be positioned no more than a foot apart from each other as the cod prefer to take lures very close to the sea bed.

The easiest method of fixing muppets to the line is to use a blood loop (illustrated in Chapter 20); do not make it a big loop – about two inches is ideal. Select a largish hook, say 4/0, and pass the loop through the eye. (With small-eye hooks or thick line this will be difficult or impossible. Find a hook with a bigger eye). The loop is then passed

over the point of the hook and pulled tight. The hook will be held firmly in position.

To fix on the muppet, make a tiny nick in the point of the head and force the hook-point downwards, through the opening. It is important that the hole should be very small and the muppet difficult to pull on since it is this gripping action that holds the muppet in place up the hook and stops it falling round the hookpoint to inhibit hook penetration. The muppet is pushed just above the hook eye.

When muppets were introduced in the mid-1970s only the red and green ones appeared to catch fish. Years later black emerged as the killing colour, while at the time of writing blue is the only colour to have. These changes of preference are a perverse business – after all, no cod ever gets the chance to learn from its mistakes . . .

Rubber eels on very short hooklengths can be substituted for the muppets – indeed, they are better if pollack are the main target. But think of the cost of each lost set of tackle before you lower them down . . .

If you are pirk fishing with a multi-hook rig I strongly recommend line of not less than 50lb and as high as 80lb for the terminal gear. This will have the strength to withstand the shock of two big fish diving in opposite directions – something that many pirk anglers have experienced to their cost.

Pirk fishing over very rough wrecks can take a heavy toll of lures and you should take at least a dozen lures on each trip. Some take twice that many and still come back empty.

Should you get fastened up on a wreck with heavy line while drifting, do not simply hang on to the rod and reel and watch the tip get forced down against the side of the boat. Even the most robust of rods can be smashed in half. You need

The angler is stuck on the bottom and is using a piece of wood with the snagged line wrapped around it to break free – much safer than using limbs or the rod.

something to wrap the line round to withstand the pressure until it is broken by the action of the drifting boat. If you have a thick fishing coat on you can take several turns of line around your arm. Do not do this on a thinly covered arm or you could injure yourself. The best is to have a short piece of wood to hand.

Feathers

To many anglers, feathers are merely a device for catching mackerel for bait. They are much more versatile. Small and medium-size fish will take them on their own and often the baited feather is a very successful method. Which type of feather is the most effective is very much a matter of regional preference – the fishes' as well as the anglers'. The traditional coloured feather is seldom the best type, since when wet it disappears into a thin wisp. Much better are the glitter and flashing type. My candidate for a universal catcher is the silver Daylite feather. Not only are they very good for mackerel, whiting and small codling; pollack and coalfish will go for them too. Glittery ones tied from Mylar tubing can also be good, as can the traditional white fluffy feather. It is often a case of discovering which type works best at a particular venue and then making that the first choice (while retaining others as a second choice).

Baiting feathers might seem a contradiction in that it is neither one thing nor the other, but rather than worry about the correctness of the combination have a fish with it, for it can be very effective for small to medium-size fish. Rig up feathers in the normal way with the sinker at the bottom of the flight. Put small pieces of bait on the hook so that the feather is not obscured. Try bits of mackerel or worm, or a bit of shellfish. You can jig the feathers normally as for mackerel, just a little bit to give the bait movement, or forget all about the lure aspect of the feathers and fish them static. Sometimes none, one, or all three methods work. It may not offer much in the way of glamour fishing but it is certainly a useful trick for the club and match angler.

THE FISH

After all the information on how to get afloat, tackle up and prepare for the business proper, it is now time to get to grips with the fish. Biology and lifestyle have been dealt with only insofar as they are relevant to catching and identifying the species; the prime subject is the business of getting a hook in the quarry.

Whatever the species, the basic rule is to think of the food the fish is after, and where that food will be. This is not easy since we cannot see what is happening in the water. What can help is an understanding of the type of ground that holds the regular foods of the different species.

I have purposely started with cod, and made it a very comprehensive chapter, not only because cod is without question the number one target of boat anglers but also because its movement and feeding patterns typify fish in general.

28 Cod

The cod is the most sought-after fish in the sea for the boat angler. Only in a few isolated areas of Wales and the West Country does cod not form the backbone of boat sport for much of the year. It is a popular fish and one I cannot ever recall anyone ever wishing he hadn't caught – which is saying something special, given the fickle taste of sea anglers. It gives me great pleasure to write about cod, which is why I wrote a whole book on the subject several years ago.

Cod grow very fast. A three-year-old fish will average 5lb, and packing on so much weight in such a short time is evidence of a voracious appetite. Cod will eat whenever there is food about, filling their stomachs to bursting point with whatever they fancy – but not with whatever comes along. Greedy they may be, but it is a selective greed. This is where some boat anglers make a fundamental mistake, subscribing to the idea that if a cod is hungry it will eat anything.

The type of ground cod inhabit is very varied. They will adapt to anything, but it is usually connected with what they wish to feed on. If their food is small fish or shrimps, the regular choice of smaller cod, they will be hunting over sandy ground where this type of food is found. If they are chasing slightly larger fish, crabs or shellfish, they will hunt over the rough ground that these creatures inhabit. Big cod living on a diet of substantial-sized fish go for the areas of broken ground where vulnerable fish will try to hide. This includes wrecks, the most consistent home of large cod.

An additional factor in the search for cod is their annual breeding migration cycle. This seasonal movement of the fish overrides feeding considerations. Cod have several major breeding grounds around the British Isles but all are outside the range of the angler. Once the cod take off for breeding, the angler will not see them again for several months.

The habits of cod vary in different parts

Light lures are a productive and fun method of catching summer cod.

of Britain, but the following generalisations are worth remembering. Cod are not sexually mature until they are about four years old or 7lb plus, so fish smaller than this are subject to different movement patterns and are not inclined to take off to spawning grounds. This is why smaller cod can be caught for most of the year, while the larger fish are found only from early summer to late winter. During the spring period the larger fish are away on the spawning grounds.

When large cod return from spawning they will be lean and their flesh soft. They will begin to feed ravenously, first appearing well offshore and then gradually coming closer inshore as the water cools down until, by December and January, very large cod may appear almost within casting distance of the shore angler. This feeding continues until late February or early March, when they take off to the spawning grounds again. They may leave earlier if food close inshore disappears – this can happen in periods of very cold weather, when the shrimps, crabs, and smaller fish move out to deeper and warmer water.

Cold will affect the movement of all cod on two counts. First, cod prefer a sea temperature of between 1° and 5°C. Small

Winter time, and the bigger cod will come inshore to feed up prior to spawning.

fish will tolerate slightly warmer weather, up to 10°C which is why codling will often come close inshore in late summer, but no size of fish will tolerate very cold water and 0°C is the absolute lower limit of endurance. The fish will die at 2 degrees below freezing point. These figures are for the temperature of the water at the sea bed where the cod are feeding; the air temperature gives only a slight indication of the temperature down below. It is worth remembering that in deep water the temperature between winter and summer hardly varies more than a degree or two.

The second influence of cold on cod movement is the effect it has on the food that the cod have come inshore to feed on. Prolonged icy weather may drive the cod further offshore as they follow the shrimps and little fish that are fleeing the plummeting water temperature.

From this collection of facts about the annual movement and the feeding preferences of cod, you can build up a picture of where the fish are going to be at any time of the year. We will start with early summer.

The sexually mature fish will have begun to return inshore from the breeding grounds to feed up. The immature fish will also have been offshore, following the food chain. The first target fish in late spring and early summer are fish in the 2–5lb range and you can expect to take them quite close inshore, since the water will still be very cold after winter, in spite of any warmth in the air from spring sunshine.

The ground they will be on can be very varied, though usually it is fairly broken, with stones, a bit of weed or ledges, the habitat of the food the cod is searching for – shrimps, crabs, and the like.

The first technique to try for these spring fish is bait fishing, with worm, either by boat-casting or with a simple one or two hook flowing trace. If you are over broken ground anchoring up will be advisable as drifting with bait over rough ground can result in a lot of lost tackle.

Lure fishing is worth trying, with a flight of muppets and a pirk on the bottom, or baited feathers. If you can get early peeler crab that may also be worth a try, since many of the smaller cod will be feeding exclusively on crabs. By midsummer the bigger cod will have begun to return from the spawning grounds and will be coming into the deeper-water marks, over rougher ground, and over wrecks. These fish can still be caught on worm baits, but cod over 10lb begin to feed more exclusively on whole fish food and worm baits are snatched by the smaller fish. Lure fishing comes into its own for these better fish, and the standard muppet-and-pirk technique is more selective for finding the better fish.

By autumn the bigger fish will have moved a little closer inshore, but the really big fish will still be hugging the wrecks and deeper water. Better cod will only start to come closer inshore when the sea gets colder in early winter, since the larger cod are less tolerant than small fish to a rise in water temperature. The very big cod will come closest to the shore between December and February, when they will have a last feeding spree before growing their roes and taking off for the spawning ground in March to commence the whole migratory pattern again.

If you want to keep some of your cod for eating, gut them as soon as possible after capture and wash them out thoroughly. The flesh will be fouled by the contents of the stomach within hours, particularly in warm weather.

Remember that cod feed hard on the bottom virtually all of the time, rising in the water only when chasing herring or sprat shoals or when swimming over wrecks. Keep baits or lures on the bottom and never go above 3 feet from the sea bed.

29   Tope and Dogs

In this chapter I cover all the commonly caught doggie types, from tope through smooth hounds, bull huss, spurdog and lesser spotted dogs. The coverage each species will get mirrors its popularity among boat anglers.

Tope

Tope are one of the few fish that boat anglers go after purely for their sporting attributes. The flesh of a tope has little kitchen appeal and most are returned alive.

Suitable traces for catching tope in the traditional over-the-back style are described in Chapter 20. Boat-casting is a successful method of tope fishing and the boat-casting trace described in Chapter 25 can be modified for the purpose. If your main line is between 15 and 20lb BS you will need a substantial length of 50lb shock leader both to withstand the impact of casting and to act as a buffer against any abrasion of the line by the rough skin of the tope. Three times the length of your rod is a good average length of leader for boat-casting for tope. An additional advantage of a long leader is that once the fish is near the boat the extra length of 50lb line can be used to haul it alongside the boat before it is lifted in.

When you lock the bait into the ground by means of the wired sinker, set the reel in free spool and put the ratchet on. If you haven't got a ratchet, or it is not strong enough to withstand the pull of the current, tighten up the spool tension nut until no more line goes out. It is imperative that the slipping clutch on the reel is set properly, or a little on the slack side, to accommodate the searing runs a hooked fish will make.

Irrespective of whether you boat-cast for tope or fish in the conventional style, do not allow the fish to run with the bait for too long. There was a time when the style for tope fishing was to wait until the fish had swallowed the bait before striking, but this

Tope respond well to a rubby-dubby trail – this one is mackerel pulped up in a bucket with a spar of wood. Tie a net over the top of the bucket and lower it down to the sea bed. Jerk the bucket periodically to keep the trail streaming out.

just results in gut-hooked fish which are almost impossible to release.

When the run starts it will often be a couple of short rapid bursts, then off on a definite run. As soon as the run proper starts lock the reel into gear and just hold on. The tope will hook itself when its powerful run is suddenly halted by the locked reel. Don't try to bully the fish into the boat, but let it career up and down the sea until it gets so tired that it can be led to the side of the boat. Since this is the end of the fight, there is no need to lift the fish into the boat if it is only lip-hooked.

Have a pair of hook forceps or strong pliers handy and get a colleague to hold the fish steady by the dorsal fin and tail while you prise the hook out by gripping it with the implement to hand and shaking vigorously. If unhooking is not that simple or you wish to get the tope in the boat for weighing or photographing you need a pair of very strong gloves. I use heavy rubberised industrial gloves. Grab the dorsal fin and the tail and heave the fish aboard. If you want to weigh it the best method is to have a sling made of trawl netting. Do not poke spring balances into the gills; even tying a tope up by the tail could lead to damage.

The tope season varies around the country but generally starts in early May and continues into autumn. All the big fish are females and if you want to catch a tope at maximum weight then go out in late May

Once unhooked, a tope can be safely handled if it is firmly grasped by the tail and the large fin near the gills.

and early June just before the tope are about to drop their pups. Tope do not lay eggs, but bring offspring into the world like humans.

The location of tope grounds also varies from region to region, but they are not lovers of deep water and do not as a rule like rough ground. Their food is almost exclusively fish and these are the baits that you must use to catch tope. There is some regional difference in the best tope baits, but all the following are worth trying.

A mackerel strip or a small joey mackerel is a favourite bait. Take a full fillet off the side of a large, fresh mackerel, or use the head, backbone and guts which are left after two fillets have been removed. If you use whole mackerel or the head and guts, hook the bait through its mouth, passing the hook through both the upper and lower jaw. If you only push the hookpoint through the tough upper jaw the mouth will open up and act as a drogue in the tide.

A popular bait in the south-east of England is portions of eel. The eel used is the common river eel, not conger, and chunks 4 or 5 inches long are used. Nick the piece of eel lightly through the skin and it will withstand casting.

Smooth Hounds

These fish are rather limited in their distribution around Britain. They have a preference for warmer water than tope and are seldom caught north of Anglesey on the west coast or East Anglia on the east coast. The main area for catching them is the south-east, particularly the Thames and its associated estuaries, and along the south coast, where they shoal up in huge packs off

One way to hook a pouting deadbait for tope. The hooks are attached Pennell-rig-style, explained in Chapter 20.

Hampshire, providing fun sport for most summer months.

Smooth hounds do not require a heavy wire trace but they have powerful denticle crushing teeth, rather like those of the ray family, so some form of protection against biting or grinding through the hooklength is needed. The simplest method is to use line of 35–40lb BS for the hook length, but you can use light-gauge wire if you wish. Smooth hounds feed almost exclusively on crabs – hard, soft and all textures in between. Your bait must be crab-based and the simplest is standard peeler crab. They feed both in daylight and at night, but in darkness will come closer inshore and are often more voracious.

Smooth hounds respond well to boat-casting techniques, but you can also catch them by conventional styles of fishing over the side of the boat. They tend to prefer clean ground and do not like any great depth of water. They are a lively fish in everything they do, and once they are hooked they will tear off into the tide, so a correct clutch setting is essential. They do not grow to any great size and one that tops 10lb is a good fish. For this reason it is more fun to fish for smooth hounds with light tackle, and tackle rated between 8 and 15lb is ideal.

Two species of the hound are caught in British waters, the smooth hound and the starry smooth hound. The only superficial difference between the two is that the starry smooth hound has white star-like blotches on its back. This is by far the most common type. There is no difference in the approach to catching either type.

It is not difficult for the untrained eye to confuse smooth hounds with small tope, particularly since both swim over the same type of ground. Large tope do not normally go for the crab baits that you will be using for smooth hounds, but smaller males may do so. The quickest method of telling them apart is by the stars on the back of the very common starry smooth hound. The tope has none. Should you suspect that you have caught one of the rarer plain smooth hounds, look at the tail fin. The tope has a square chunk cut out of it, the smooth hound has a smooth tail.

Bull Huss

Bull Huss (also known as the greater spotted dog fish or the nursehound) is not a species that excites anglers to any great degree, since its action is little more than that of a large lesser spotted doggie. It is taken on fish baits, and while it will be picked up on the smooth ground populated by other members of the dog family it often prefers to feed over stones and rocky ground.

The huss has not got any powerful cutting teeth but has a rough skin and the stubby teeth that can grind through line. Use the 35 or 40lb line recommended for smooth hounds. Talk of tackle is a little academic, in that the huss is very rarely purposely fished for. They are most likely to turn up while the angler is fishing for ray, small reef conger or tope.

It is possible to confuse small huss with large lesser spotted dogs. Two clues are the colour – the huss is a much deeper brown than the common doggie – and the presence of much larger spots on the huss, amounting to large dark brown blotches.

Spurdog

The spurdog is pursued less for its sporting qualities than for its eating. This is the fish which is described as rock salmon. Spurdog roam the waters around Britain during summer in huge and very dense shoals, and despite commercial pressure on the stock, still seem to come in great numbers.

Spurdog like this are often in dense packs which feed in a frenzy.

They are similar in shape to the smooth hound and tope, but can be easily identified by the presence of a sharp thorn or spur in front of each of the two dorsal fins. Beware of these spines while handling the dog, since they will inflict serious injury if they puncture your skin while the fish is thrashing about in the boat.

The spurdog grows into double figures and at this size offers a good account of itself on light tackle. Unfortunately, spurs average less than this, and the huge packs that anglers tangle with are fish between 4 and 8lb. They can offer some pleasure to the match angler who wishes to amass a great weight of fish, or for those who have some commercial or culinary reason for wanting to kill more than one fish.

These pack fish will feed in a frenzy on any fish bait, notably mackerel chunks. The fish has a habit of spinning around once hooked and for this reason short hook-lengths are advisable, and no more than two. If you attach the hooklengths by a clip system you will be able to detach and change those which inevitably get snarled up. Medium weight wire is the best material for hooklengths; wire of about 30lb BS will resist the sharp teeth of the spurdog.

Lesser Spotted Dogfish

The humble little doggie, loved by no one, hated by many, is small, takes baits intended for other species with such enthusiasm that the target fish escapes capture, tangles up terminal tackle and swims all over the place. It is happy with the rough and the smooth, deep and shallow, will take just about any bait and has no fighting or eating qualities. To their own dishonour, many anglers cruelly unhook the little fellow, thinking more of the hook than the fish.

30 Pollack and Coalfish

These two species are linked genetically and also to a large extent in the way that anglers approach them. For reasons which I shall explain, pollack present the better sporting prospect of the two.

Pollack

Pollack spend a lot of their time in shallow water. They will lie motionless in weed or just on top of it while small school fish swim by, then snap out and grab the hapless passer-by. Pollack are fierce-fighting fish and respond well to light tackle.

On inshore marks they appear in spring and will stay until autumn, when they disappear into deeper water for the winter months in preparation for spawning, which takes place in very deep offshore waters. The angler can exploit this preference for shallow ground by searching for pollack over reefs and around rock cliffs that plunge into deep water. Pollack are not by nature a deep-water fish and do not hug the bottom like for instance, cod. They can be found feeding on or near the bottom, but are just as happy feeding at mid-water or even higher up.

To find pollack, if you know that they are in the general area, look for the signs of rough ground on a chart, on the echo sounder or by islands or rocks that push up out of the water. Pinnacle rock is a real favourite of pollack, and on this type of ground they will lie motionless up the side of the pinnacle waiting for some unsuspecting little fish to pass by.

Pollack are mainly fish feeders, and angling tactics should reflect this. The most popular method of catching pollack is to use artificial lures. The rubber eel is the best known and most successful and should be fished in the flying-collar manner described in Chapter 20. You can also jig a flight of two or three rubber eels fished on short hooklengths.

Spinning is a very productive method for pollack in shallow water; the ubiquitous eel can be used or any one of a host of bar-shaped lures. Everyone has his favourites: mine are Abu Krill lures, Cebar sprat lures, and the ever-popular Toby.

Work as near to the rock and weed as you dare, for it is in this ground that the pollack will be waiting. Your clutch must be adjusted correctly with the star drag set so that no matter how abrupt the pull line will come off the reel and not be broken. Pollack will make a fierce run when first hooked, heading back into the weed or rock where he feels safe but the line decidedly isn't! When spinning for pollack use line of not less than 25lb immediately in front of the spinner. Pollack have a row of raspy teeth along the inside roof of the mouth and they can grind through thin line in the course of a battle. All you need do is have a 12 inch section of the heavier line to act as a guard, with line of 15lb BS or whatever as the reel line.

If you want to try catching pollack on bait the only one worth a serious try is fish strip, preferably mackerel. You can fish it on the bottom or under a float. Float fishing is particularly useful when you wish to drift

Drifting close in under rocky headlands – the ideal ground to find pollack and coalfish.

in close to a rocky edge and drift a bait over the top of a weedbed. Live sandeel is a superb pollack bait if you can get hold of it, and it can be fished either static or in the flying-collar method.

A method that occasionally works very well for pollack is to freeline a ragworm through the water. You will need light line, and all the weight that is required is a swan shot or a swivel. Hook the ragworm once through the head and just lower it into the water to sink, with the worm wriggling tantalisingly in the current as it slowly falls.

If you want to try for a really big pollack, the best place to go is a deep-water wreck in the West County. This is where all the biggest pollack are caught, by the flying-collar rubber-eel method or with two or three eels fished paternoster-style. Curiously, while there are wrecks that hold pollack in many other parts of the British Isles, it is only off Devon and Cornwall that double-figure pollack appear regularly.

Whatever the method or location, fish on the drift, since this will add movement to the presentation.

Coalfish

This is an enigmatic species. When they are small, they populate the inshore waters of northern parts of the British Isles in great numbers. The shoals are so dense that they

Under the cliffs – perfect ground for hunting pollack.

will show up as a dark mass on an echo sounder. These fish are no more than an irritant, for they will seldom weigh more than 2lb and they hit lures and feathers as soon as they go down.

Yet, in spite of the vastness of stocks of small coalfish, large coalfish are very rarely caught by anglers. The areas that year after year produce the little fish never offer anything above 3lb. I suspect that the larger coalfish have a liking for deeper, darker water, and that they feed on mid-water food fish such as herring and sprat. So not only are anglers fishing in the wrong areas for large coalfish, but almost certainly fish at the wrong depth too.

The only ground where big coalfish are a real possibility is wrecks and, as with pollack, the West Country wrecks offer the best chance. The period from December to March is the prime time for the really big specimens.

The methods that work for pollack will work for coalfish, except that coalies prefer slightly deeper levels in the water than pollack. As a guide, think of them as sitting between the cod which are hard on the sea bed and the pollack which are in mid-water.

Telling the two apart is not as difficult as is sometimes suggested. Coalfish have a very shiny, almost varnished sheen to them; the back is a faint dark green and the upper and lower lips line up. The lower jaw of the pollack protrudes and the fish is often of a bronzy colour with a slightly dull finish.

31 Conger

Congers live in rough ground or wrecks where they can set up their own territory and use it as a base from which to make sorties. Their body is very flexible and they will back into crevices and under ledges and lie motionless for hours on end. Where they inhabit the broken holes in old stone piers you can actually see them doing this.

They prefer to feed at night, when they will wander over the ground in search of crabs, small fish and anything they can catch. Night time, even in deep water, is the best time for serious conger fishing, but they will still take a bait offered in daylight if it is dropped on their nose in front of their home.

Fishing for big eels is usually done well offshore in charter boats and the skipper will position his boat in such a way as to allow the maximum number of rods to fish in the wreck or just alongside it. They are not a hard-fighting fish as such; the struggle comes from trying to prise the eel from its home or prevent it bolting back into it. That is why very heavy tackle is needed to take on the bigger eels that live in wrecks – 50lb class rods and reels are essential.

Eels prefer to feed around slack water, or at dusk and dawn in shallow water. Your terminal tackle for big fish must be the short, heavy-duty trace described in Chapter 20. Do not skimp on the strength of the final 6 inches before the hook, since congers have pincer-like teeth.

Good baits are a bloody fillet of mackerel, the head, backbone and gut of a mackerel left after taking two fillets off, or just the head itself. A recently killed small pouting is

also a good conger bait. Fish the bait hard on the bottom and engage the reel gears. The first sign of a bite will be a thump-thump, followed by a pause. Conger are not fast-taking fish and what often happens is that the eel clamps its teeth around the body of the bait (that first thump-thump) before either turning it and beginning to swallow it on the site or dragging it back towards its lair. You can disengage the reel and let the eel take a little line to encourage it to take the bait in its mouth.

Either way, as soon as the second thumping starts, engage the reel, tighten up slowly but firmly, and, when you feel the fish on the end, arc the rod high in the sky and begin reeling for all you are worth. If you get more than a handful of turns in without the rod being savagely dragged down you have missed the bite and almost certainly your bait will have been chomped to ribbons. If the eel is hooked you must pile on the pressure to keep the eel away from its home. When it gets into mid-water the fight may completely go out of the eel, or it may attempt to dive back down to the sea bed. As long as your clutch is correctly set you have few problems.

Beware of the conger on the surface, for it may make a last dive for freedom. When it is gaffed and brought aboard have some means of controlling it already to hand. A charter boat that regularly fishes for big eels will have a large bin with a lid on it just for lively eels. If you are in a small boat, have a strong sack ready. Attaching the hook-length by a clip system means that you will not have to unhook the conger while it is thrashing about. Beware of the conger's jaws and teeth – both are vicious and the conger may well make a snap at unwary fingers. With a clip system, you can simply detach the hooklength and put on a new one.

Fishing for smaller eels over reefs and rocky ground is much less demanding, and, if the truth be known, a lot less interesting. These reef fish do not offer much at all in the way of a fight and are little more than a mild amusement to the serious conger hunter.

32 Plaice

It is difficult to pin down why catching a big plaice gives such pleasure since by no stretch of angling licence could I say that they are fierce fighters. It is probably the elusiveness of the big fish that makes them so prized.

Since plaice are flatfish, the ground where they are to be found has got to be flattish. It need not be pure, driven sand, since plaice have a liking for mussel beds, but do not look for them on rocky ground. Ideally, try to find the edge of banks, where the plaice will roam in search of food scoured out of the sides of the sandbank by the tidal flow. Do not look for deep water; plaice are very happy to feed in water so shallow that the boat might ground.

Plaice feed on shellfish – notably mussels – and small shrimplike creatures. These, however, are not the best baits. Worm is by far the most universal catcher of plaice – whether lugworm or ragworm seems to make little difference. The other bait that can account for good plaice is sandeel, fished either live, or in pieces, or in long fillets taken from the whole side of an eel.

There are several approaches to tackling up for plaice. The simple flowing trace with two trailing hooks below the weight is effective, as is a wire spreader rig. These two rigs are unbeatable for taking a quantity of small-to-medium-size plaice.

If you are after a big fish, and presuming you believe them to be on the ground you are fishing (there are very few places in Britain left where big plaice do abound), you could try a very long flowing trace. By long I mean between 12 and 20 feet.

This may sound grotesquely unmanageable – it is not easy – but on such a long trace in an area of strong tidal flow the bait will be made to sway, rise and fall with the current in a most tantalising manner. This is the system used on that famous plaice mark the Skerries Bank, off Dartmouth, and it can pay handsome dividends elsewhere too. The Skerries plaice respond to slivers of sandeel, or very long slivers of squid. You may try either yourself or stay faithful to worm.

It is impossible to cast with a trace as long

Plaice will sometimes respond to a bait that has got coloured beads suspended on the hook line.

Standing up in a small boat to net a fish needs great care and should never be done when there is any swell.

as this. Lower the bait in the water and let it stream away from the boat. When the full trace is lying across the tide, pay out the sinker slowly and let it drop down to the bottom. This way will prevent hooklength and sinker tangling. When the tackle is retrieved the trace line must be handlined in when the sinker reaches the top of the rod.

This is a time-consuming rig and will attract smaller plaice as well as larger ones. For this reason, if small and medium plaice are responding to it you would be advised to revert to a more manageable length.

Plaice are inquisitive creatures and will often go for an attractor just above the hook. The two most popular forms are a flashing-blade spinner and coloured beads.

The flashing-blade spinner is no more than a bar spinner (Mepps, Droppen-type) with the treble hook snipped off. The hook is attached by a very short piece of nylon to the loop that once held the treble and the hooklength made up to the desired length with a section of line between the top of the spinner and the sinker clip.

With beads, try white or luminous green ones. Let three or four slide freely up and down the hooklength. Whether beads or a bar spinner do contribute to the catch rate is very difficult to prove. Certainly a lot of anglers swear by them, and I could write a whole chapter on this subject – but I won't.

Do not be in a hurry to strike at plaice bites. They are a fish that are not easily put off by a hook. It is not unreasonable to suggest that more plaice are missed by early striking than by not striking at all. In spite of hooking themselves, plaice will often only do this in the lip. For this reason have a large landing net to hand for lifting quality fish into the boat. There have been tragic cases of big plaice falling off the hook just as they were being swung into a boat.

33 Thornback and Other Rays

Thornbacks are the rays that anglers most frequently come into contact with. I shall mention other types at the end of this chapter, but a lot of what applies to thornies – or roker, as they are sometimes called – is applicable to all members of the ray family.

The distribution of rays stretches from the west of Scotland all around the English coast to the Humber, where they become scarce. Their food is crabs and shellfish, and any small fish they can catch or grub out. They have no teeth but powerful grinding gums that can crush hard crabs, light line or unsuspecting fingers.

The ground they find this food on varies from sand and mud through shingle to coarse gravel. They don't mind a few rocks and bigger stones but their body shape is designed for gliding over smooth ground so they will avoid patches of rough ground. They winter in deep water and come inshore in the spring to breed, which is when anglers begin to catch them.

The natural food of the thornback is crab, but fish pieces make a very successful angling bait for them. The hook need not be over-large, reflecting the size of the bait used. This suggests a hook from 4/0 to 6/0, and it need not be a heavyweight one. While the ray cannot bite through line, it can abrade it, so make your hooklengths in nylon of 35–40 lb or lightweight wire.

Uptide fishing is a very successful method of catching rays, because of the shallow water they populate and their habit of plopping down on a bait and engulfing it without the need for striking. If fishing downtide of the boat, put the reel in free spool and click the ratchet into gear. If line is pulled off the ratchet tighten up the spool tension until the pull of the tide alone is not strong enough to carry the line away. Whichever method you employ, a single hook will keep things tidy.

Rays do not make long runs normally, but there will be a sudden short rapid burst from the ratchet as the fish lands on top of the line and drags some off the reel. If you strike at this point you may well miss the ray or hook it in the wing, since this first indication is probably caused by the body of the fish and not its jaws. Give the fish time to reposition itself on the bait and get it in its mouth – something that experience teaches rather than a book. Rays are not 'snatch and drop it' takers so there is little risk of losing the fish because of your patience in waiting for the bite to develop fully. When there are more pulls on the line you can be confident that the bait is in the fish's mouth, at which time pick the rod up, reel furiously, and then when you feel the weight of a fish strike high and hard. This sounds very precise, but in fact a lot of thornbacks hook themselves if left.

Peeler crab is a good all-round thornie bait, as are strips of fresh mackerel, frozen sandeels and even sprats. They will take worm, but it is not mainline ray bait.

Other rays caught by anglers include the small-eyed or painted ray, the spotted, the blonde, the cuckoo and the sting ray. These are restricted in their location, but the angling baits and techniques are similar to those used for thornbacks.

34 Bass

Although often thought of as the shore angler's fish, a great deal of boat-angling effort is spent on chasing bass. The prime requirements for bass fishing are shallow ground and stealth. Bass will roam over a wide variety of ground in the search for food and are just as happy grubbing about in sand for sandeels and crabs as on the roughest of rock chasing small fry.

Bass like plenty of movement in the water and some of the more famous bass marks, such as Beachy Head and the Thames estuary, have very fierce tides. Another area of fast water always worth trying is the area of an estuary bar. This is where the river meets the sea proper. There is often a build-up of sand which, while it may not be uncovered, forms a considerable hump which the water breaks over. The sandeels which populate these banks are scoured out by the strong current. Bass know this and lie in wait for anything that gets dislodged.

Smaller bass are shoaling fish, and only when they get above 6lb do they start to spread out and become lone hunters. There are two fishing methods for bass: spinning or bait fishing. The former is the more popular and successful.

The deadliest form of spinning is not strictly spinning at all, it is trolling, which is done at a much slower retrieve rate than with a spinner or bar lure. The rubber eel is the king of this style of fishing and, if you want greatly to increase your chances of

bass when trolling, use a live sandeel instead of a rubber one.

Always do this type of bass fishing on the drift, which will allow you to cover more ground and give an extra bit of movement to your lure. Bass are very shy fish and will disperse quickly at the sound of a boat engine or even the slapping of a boat riding at anchor. Approach the bass mark from uptide, cut your engine a couple of hundred yards from the spot you wish to fish, and drift in on the tide.

While you can troll over known bass marks, always keep you eyes alert to sea birds working over a shoal of sprat or whitebait. If this occurs over shallow ground there could well be a shoal of bass underneath the sprat, pushing them to the surface, which is why the birds are so excited.

As well as eels, I like the Cebar lure, the Toby lure, and one of the most deadly bass lures of all – the Rapala plug. Whatever the lure, work it at various depths and speeds, since bass are liable to be working at all sorts of depths, according to where the food is.

If you want to try bait fishing for bass, then let the boat drift if the ground is smooth enough. Live sandeel is head and shoulders above any other bass bait. Next comes peeler crab and ragworm. Bass have no teeth, so there is no need to have a heavier line for the hooklength, but I would not recommend going below 15lb.

35   Other Species

Ling

A member of the cod family, ling are most frequently caught from wrecks or very rough ground. Pirking is the most widely used method of catching them and all the tactics and pirks suitable for cod will also take ling. If you are fishing a wreck and wish to increase your chances of catching a ling, bait the pirk treble with a substantial piece of mackerel. This works wonders for ling, and also deters cod slightly.

Baiting the pirk is always worth trying should your wreck hold few cod, or if the stamp of fish seems on the small side. If you are fishing over broken reef ground on the drift, bait up one of your muppets or feathers to test out whether ling are about – though the ling that inhabit these reefs are often small fish of little interest for anything.

Small ling like this can be very prolific – and annoying – on offshore reefs.

Haddock

Sadly, haddock are nowhere near as widespread as ten years ago. A few fish are caught in the Devon and Cornwall end of the English Channel, otherwise you must go to the northern part of the North Sea, above Yorkshire, or the west coast of Scotland and the Hebridean Islands. I enjoy catching haddock, and try to get in at least one trip a year for them.

I have found that shellfish is the best bait followed by lugworm. The scallop clam is the best bait, and if you cannot get (or afford) the full animal a rummage in the rubbish skip of a clam processor will produce masses of clam fringes, the tougher fibrous part of the clam left on the shell by the processing. Pile plenty of these fringes on a hook and lash them on with fine-gauge elastic cotton. Cockles and mussels also work well. A bonus of shellfish baits is that, unlike lugworm, other species of fish such as coalfish and codling do not take them eagerly.

Try baited feathers for small-to-medium haddock, especially when fishing on the drift. A final tip: the stomach of a haddock is packed with strong smelling bile. Gut and wash haddock thoroughly as soon as possible.

Turbot

Turbot have always been rare and are getting rarer. The first requisite for catching turbot is a mark where they are known to be, and in this you must be guided by either the charter skipper or sound personal knowledge. The turbot is a fish eater and baits should be long, thin strips of mackerel, preferably the silvery bits from the belly, or a live or dead sandeel. If you have some

Turbot, king of the flatfish and getting scarcer every year for anglers.

greater sandeels or launces, you can cut long fillets from these.

The terminal gear is like the long trace used for plaice, but make the hooklength of 35lb BS since the turbot has a rough mouth that could chafe through thin line.

Whiting

Very common all around Britain, whiting seldom evoke any greater response from anglers than fondness – always provided that the fish are not taking baits intended for something else and are a respectable size.

Whiting are not averse to taking a bait slightly off the bottom, so for small-to-medium size fish you can tackle up with a flowing trace with a boom above. Do not make the hooklengths long – you will gain nothing from it and the skittish way whiting dart about can cause awful tangles.

Mackerel is a very good bait for whiting. I like little chunks the size of a sugar cube or just bigger rather than strips, since the whiting tear at the bait and can drag it off the hook, giving a bite but not having the hook in the mouth. Lugworm tipped with small cubes of mackerel is another good bait. Baited feathers are always worth a try for small whiting.

Bream

Very limited in their distribution, bream are restricted to parts of mid-Wales and Hampshire and Sussex. The bream like fairly shallow ground, reefs and even pinnacle rock. Fish a single hook on a short wire boom above the sinker, so that the bait just clears the sea bed.

Best baits are fish-based – cubes of mackerel or squid. Worm will catch bream but also attracts hordes of unwanted fish such as pouting, little wrasse and coalfish.

Dabs

Prolific, sweet-tasting and catchable for most of the year, the little dab has no sporting qualities but is a fun species to catch when nothing else is about. Like the plaice, dabs respond to coloured beads on the hook length. If quantity is required fish a two-or three-boom steel paternoster spreader or flowing trace with three hooks below the sinker.

Worm baits reign supreme but lug tipped with mackerel will sometimes pick out the better fish.

Wrasse

Not a fish readily associated with boat fishing, wrasse can nevertheless be very widespread on shallow reefs, and the same rock edges that produce pollack will produce wrasse. Crab will pick out the bigger fish while worm will take smaller wrasse. In spite of their reputation for not feeding on fish, don't be surprised if you get them pirking, feathering or spinning. Fish a single boom above the sinker with the bait a few inches clear of the sea bed.

Catfish

Catfish are restricted to north-eastern England and Scotland. My only reason for mentioning this ugliest of all fish is to warn against its teeth and jaws, which are wickedly vicious. They will chomp through wellingtons given half a chance and do not die easily. . .

Weever

Weevers are sometimes caught over sandy or muddy ground when fishing for small

Catfish – caught in northern waters around Britain and armed with a mean set of teeth.

flatties or feathering hard on the bottom. The venom from the spines is not lethal, but the pain is extremely intense. There is no antidote for it and no reason to go to hospital unless other symptons occur, such as dizziness or fainting. Should one come in board do not touch it, but kill it immediately with a long, blunt instrument.

Mackerel

I could not write about the fish which boat anglers catch without saying something about the mackerel, around which so much of our success revolves. It is not a sporting species as such, but it is a popular and very successful bait – so much so that catching them is a serious business.

Traditional gaily coloured feathers are not the most efficient mackerel feathers. I much prefer the silvery fabric type known as Daylite feathers, but I always carry a range of mackerel feathers since the fish respond to different types in different areas.

A good sign that mackerel are about is sea birds working on the surface. Gannets and gulls will be working a tight circle, diving and splashing about on the surface as they chase the tiny sprat or whitebait that the marauding mackerel down below have chased up.

The echo sounder is another good indicator of mackerel and may also tell you at what level they are feeding. To find the level (and it may change while you are fishing), drop your feathers to the sea bed and work for a minute or two at this level. If nothing happens, wind up six turns and try again, repeating this procedure until you have covered all depths, at which stage you can begin over again or try somewhere else. If one mackerel takes, you can pause while it thrashes about in the water, since it will work the remaining feathers in a way you never could and the whole string may fill up!

If you want specialist fish like turbot then you will have to locate a skipper with a proven track record for this increasingly rare fish.

Baited feather is often a very good way of taking medium-size ling.

Epilogue

I have run out of pages. There is much more that could be said, since our sport is not an exact science but a mixture of folklore, half-truths, superstition and prejudice, stirred up with a collection of basic rules.

I hope I have set out the basic rules while at the same time providing enough of the other bits to entertain, provoke thought and set you off on your own path. I hope I have also emphasised that while fishing in a boat of your own is great fun, it brings with it much greater responsibility – to yourself, to your passengers and to those who might be called out to help you in distress.

Remember, too, that boat fishing is an evolving sport and we are continually learning, adapting and even changing ideas. All the best ideas come from the grass roots, so if you think of something different, don't just think about it – try it! If it doesn't work, bury it; if it does, tell someone else and help the evolutionary process along.

Sail on, shipmates!

Glossary

Aberdeen A lightweight style of hook made from thin wire.

Aerator An electrically powered air pump for oxygenating water.

Afto roller A type of rod ring with built-in rollers to reduce friction as the line passes over them.

Ammo eel Quick-frozen sandeel from a firm called Ammodyte.

Ashpole boom A sliding link used for attaching the sinker.

Avis boom A small standing-off plastic boom used for attaching hooklengths to the main line.

Bar A sandbank in the mouth of an estuary.

Bell sinker A conical-shaped sinker, usually made in heavy weights.

Bilge The area of a boat between the deck and the hull, which collects dirty water.

Blade spinner A revolving blade without a hook, used as an attractor.

Blow lug Small lugworm which turn to jelly when they die.

Boat-casting Casting away from the boat and holding a position on the sea bed by means of a wired sinker.

Bow The front of a boat.

Bruce anchor A plough-shaped boat anchor.

Calamari squid A small imported squid.

Cathedral hull A boat hull profile in the shape of a 'W'.

Charter boat A large boat that takes out a party of anglers on a chartered trip.

Clements boom A sliding boom for attaching the sinker to the tackle.

Clutch A device on a reel that allows line to be pulled off by the action of a fish.

Clutter Interference on the screen of an echo sounder or radar caused by plankton or very tiny fish.

Confluence of current Where two or more currents meet and cause turbulence.

Courlene A bright-orange nylon line.

Dacron A man-made thread used to make fishing line.

Displacement hull A boat which sits in water and displaces it.

Eddystone eel The brand name of a type of rubber eel.

Fathom 6 feet or slightly less than 2 metres.

Fixed-spool reel One where the line drum does not revolve, sometimes called a spinning reel.

Flashpoint Style of medium-weight hook.

Flukes The points of an anchor which dig into the ground.

French boom A stand-off boom attached to the main line and to which a hooklength is attached.

GRP Glass-reinforced plastic, another name for fibreglass.

Gunwhale The upper edge of a boat, usually pronounced 'gunnell'.

Hooklength A piece of line used for attaching a hook to the main line.

Jig A heavy piece of metal which simulates an injured fish when jerked through the water. Also known as a pirk.

Joey mackerel A colloquial term for little mackerel.

L-boom A boom similar to the French boom and used in a similar manner.

Lighting board The board slung from the rear of a boat trailer which carries the number plate and rear lights.

Lure Anything that is artificial but represents a live piece of food, usually a small fish.

Mackerel feathers Brightly dyed wisps of feather tied to hooks and used to catch mackerel and other smaller species.

Moon boots Heavily insulated boots, so nicknamed because of their similarity to the huge boots worn by astronauts.

Muppet Colloquial name for an imitation-squid lure.

Mylar A glittery thread used in making lures.

Neap The period of the month when tidal movement is slow and weak and tidal range is smallest.

Paternoster A terminal tackle in which several hooks are carried on snoods at intervals above the sinker.

Peeler crab A crab which is about to enter its regular moulting cycle and has a very thin and brittle shell.

Pirk Another name for a jig.

Planing hull One which is designed for skipping along the surface of the sea rather than riding in it.

Plug An artificial fish lure, usually made from wood or a floating material.

Ratchet The clicking device on a reel.

Red Gills A brand of soft rubber eels.

Rigs Another name for terminal tackle.

Roller rings See Aftco roller.

Rowlocks The U-shaped cups used for supporting oars. Pronounced 'rollocks'.

Slipping clutch See Clutch.

Snood Another name for the hooklength.

Split shot Small balls of lead or lead substitute with a deep cut in them which can be squeezed on the line to provide weight in the terminal tackle.

Spring tide The tides in the monthly cycle, with the greatest range and strongest flow.

Star drag Another name for the slipping clutch on a multiplier reel because the adjustment is often done with a star-shaped wheel.

Stern The rear of a boat.

Toby lure Brand name of a metal lure in the shape of a sprat.

Trace The arrangement of line and hooks at the end of the tackle.

Transom The flat rear portion of a boat to which the outboard motor is clamped.

Twisters Soft rubber imitation worms used as lures.

Undertow The force of water that passes underneath a crashing wave with equal force but in a seaward direction.

Zip slider A brand of sliding plastic boom for attaching a sinker to the terminal tackle.

Index